Depression: A Very Short Introduction

VERY SHORT INTRODUCTIONS are for anyone wanting a stimulating and accessible way into a new subject. They are written by experts, and have been translated into more than 45 different languages.

The series began in 1995, and now covers a wide variety of topics in every discipline. The VSI library now contains over 500 volumes—a Very Short Introduction to everything from Psychology and Philosophy of Science to American History and Relativity—and continues to grow in every subject area.

Very Short Introductions available now:

Available soon:

For more information visit our website

www.oup.com/vsi/

Mary Jane Tacchi and Jan Scott

DEPRESSION

A Very Short Introduction

OXFORD
UNIVERSITY PRESS

OXFORD

UNIVERSITY PRESS

Great Clarendon Street, Oxford, OX2 6DP,
United Kingdom

Oxford University Press is a department of the University of Oxford.
It furthers the University's objective of excellence in research, scholarship,
and education by publishing worldwide. Oxford is a registered trade mark of
Oxford University Press in the UK and in certain other countries

First edition published in 2017

Impression: 1

Published in the United States of America by Oxford University Press
198 Madison Avenue, New York, NY 10016, United States of America

British Library Cataloguing in Publication Data
Data available

Library of Congress Control Number: 2016947796

ISBN 978-0-19-955865-0

Printed in Great Britain by
Ashford Colour Press Ltd, Gosport, Hampshire

To Joan and Dorothy—our wonderful mothers

Contents

Preface

Depression is the most common mental disorder in the developed world. It particularly affects adults of working age and so the consequences extend beyond the problems associated with the clinical symptoms and impairments in day-to-day functioning experienced by the individual, to broader economic and societal costs. Yet, despite evidence of the real impact of depression on individuals and society, the whole subject of depression is mired in controversy. This is partly because the concept means different things to different people. Many acknowledge that states of depression are authentic but struggle to differentiate between depression as an emotion or mood state (such as dejection or sadness), depression as part of someone's (pessimistic) personality makeup, and depression as a mental disorder (sadness accompanied by symptoms such as sleep, concentration, appetite, and energy disturbances). Others accept the idea of 'clinical depression', but see it as a problem of the mind, which is regarded as the element of a person that enables them to be aware of the world and their experiences, to think, and to feel. People who focus on the mind often reject the notion of biological causes. Others still see depression as an understandable reaction to life circumstances that should therefore either be allowed to heal naturally or should only be treated with psychological and social interventions. Whilst there are some observers who claim that depression is an invention of the modern world, blame the rise of 'medicalization', and see those who promote treatments, especially the use of antidepressants, as entering some sort of conspiracy with certain factions or organizations such as the pharmaceutical industry.

To try to make sense of some of these different perspectives we have decided to use this text to discuss the evolution of the concept of depression and its treatment and also to examine some of the controversies and future directions for research. To understand the path we have taken it is helpful to offer a few observations at the outset. For example, it is useful to know that the term depression comes from the Latin *de* (down from) and *premere* (to press) and so *deprimere* translates as 'to press down'. This word gained widespread acceptance in the 19th and 20th centuries, and was increasingly used to describe mental conditions experienced by individuals who were treated in the community. However, before the word depression came into common parlance, the word melancholia had been employed. Technically, the term melancholia refers to a mental condition that is characterized by more extreme levels of depression, accompanied by physical symptoms, and sometimes by hallucinations and delusions. In the 19th century, the use of the term melancholia was more restricted, being mainly applied to individuals with severe depression that required treatment in the old asylums.

We use this evolution to help readers to understand that these different views of depression have influenced theories of the causes of depression and the nature of the treatments that may be offered. We also want to alert readers to how depression was understood by the so-called Fathers of Modern Psychiatry such as Emil Kraepelin and Sigmund Freud, whose ideas have been viewed as not only influential but also controversial.

We hope that the approach we have taken allows people to understand the context in which international approaches to classifying mental disorders were developed. The background information we provide attempts to shed light on the efforts made to distinguish clinical depression from the normal human experience of sadness on the one hand and from other severe mental disorders such as manic depression (also called bipolar disorders) or schizophrenia (also called psychotic disorders) on the other. It also highlights that drawing boundaries and developing categories for diagnosis, an approach which is widely accepted in medicine, is often derided in psychiatry. We discuss some of the reasons for these double standards and then move on to discuss theories about the causes of depression and how old-fashioned treatments for melancholia evolved into modern treatments for depression and manic depression.

Other chapters examine some of the current controversies about what treatments and therapies may work for depression and then some indications about future research are given. We finish by examining depression in society from the perspective of its global burden and economics, as well as issues such as stigma and whether people who experience mood disorders are more likely to be creative than other members of society.

We want to highlight that condensing information about the most common mental health problem on the planet into 35,000 words has been a challenge. So, this *Very Short Introduction* includes a selection of topics that we find are interesting or challenging (does depression exist?), issues that cannot be ignored (how can suicide be prevented?), and some of the themes that we think will become more talked about in the next few years (does psychotherapy change brain functioning?). It is difficult to do justice to some of these topics in a few thousand words and we have excluded many issues that you may want to know more about. It is likely that many of these topics were considered or indeed were included in the earlier drafts of the manuscript. We can only apologize if issues that are particularly important to you have ended up on the cutting-room floor.

If you are thinking of buying this *VSI* volume then it is probably sensible for us to be also clear about what this book does not include. We have not written a patient guide—you are unlikely to be able to decide from reading this book whether you have depression or a certain type of mood disorder. If you have or previously have had an episode of depression, this book is unlikely to help you determine if your experiences have been caused by a chemical imbalance in your brain or by life events or some other combination of factors. This is not the goal of what we have written about. Nor is this book a treatment manual; we do not begin to discuss what treatment best suits which person. Even more importantly, this is not a self-help book; we do not describe techniques to deal with the symptoms of depression. Lastly, a *VSI* book is not a substitute for a textbook; we are not trying to cover every theory, every type of treatment available, and every aspect of depression. Indeed, as the title suggests this is a very (very) short introduction and selective review of a complex and challenging topic.

List of illustrations

Chapter 1
A very short history of melancholia

In ancient times the word melancholia rather than the word depression was used to describe mood disorders characterized by despondency. The word melancholia probably originated in the ancient civilizations of Greece and Mesopotamia. As such, we begin by highlighting the descriptions of melancholia and theories about its causes that held sway from ancient times until about the 19th century. For more detailed accounts, readers may wish to consult some of the excellent textbooks on this topic, such as Stanley Jackson's *Melancholia and Depression* or relevant chapters of German Berrios's *The History of Mental Symptoms*.

From black bile to the Stoic philosophers

Probably the first description of melancholia as a specific disease was written by Hippocrates, a Greek physician often referred to as the Father of Medicine, who lived in the 4th century BC. Hippocrates stated that melancholia was characterized by despondency, aversion to food, sleeplessness, irritability, and restlessness. He explained the development of this state using humoralism, a theory that suggested melancholia was an illness with a physical cause, which differentiated his model from primitive theories that blamed supernatural forces. Although humoral theory had many advocates, it was Hippocrates who is especially credited with the introduction of the concept of black bile.

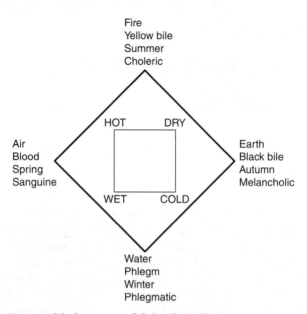

1. Diagram of the humours and their relationships.

In his book *The Nature of Man*, Hippocates described four humours within the body: black bile, yellow bile, phlegm, and blood. When all the humours were in equilibrium the body was healthy, but imbalances were thought to lead to disease. It was suggested that the humours were linked to the four elements air, water, earth, and fire (see Figure 1). Melancholia, due to an excess of black bile, was thought to be associated with autumn and with coldness and dryness. Hippocrates also recognized a condition that was akin to mania, which was described as a condition marked by periods of great excitement and overactivity. Hippocrates argued that this condition was related to an excess of yellow bile during the summer and with warm, dry air. It was proposed that treatments should target the restoration of humoral balances, which often involving purging and blood-letting.

The ideas expressed by Hippocrates were further developed in the 3rd century BC by the Greek philosopher Aristotle and his followers in a work entitled *Problemata*. This proposed that the temperature of bile was the most important factor and if it was too cold it caused 'groundless despondency'. He suggested that less severe imbalances of bile led to a melancholic temperament rather than illness, which was one of the few attempts to describe a continuum between personality and mental disorders since Plato's writings on universality. Also, Aristotle is one of the first to suggest that melancholic temperament could be associated with creativity and intellect, and he reported that it was often found in philosophers, politicians, artists, and writers.

The 1st century AD saw further developments in the theories and treatments of melancholia. For example, Soranus of Ephesus was one of the first physicians to recognize that mania and melancholia were chronic diseases associated with loss of reason. Further, he promoted the idea that treatments to improve physical health could improve mental health and that psychological interventions, such as the sound of dripping water to induce sleep, might be beneficial.

At around the same time, Rufus of Ephesus provided descriptions of melancholia that remained influential for many centuries. He noted that the people he described as melancholics were sad, gloomy, fearful, and doubting, and that their physical appearance changed during these episodes. Rufus suggested that there could be an inborn (congenital) form and an acquired form of melancholia, which is the first description of the idea that melancholia may be the final outcome of a number of different processes and could have multiple causes. Historically, his name became associated with the sacred remedy—a mixture of herbs purported to prevent melancholia.

One of the most famous Greek physicians was Galen of Pergamum (1st–2nd century AD). Galen was the physician to Marcus Aurelius and he is important because he had some influence over Roman medicine. Until his emergence, Roman society had often regarded melancholia as a punishment from the gods. In his book *On the Affected Parts*, Galen developed detailed theories of how different humoral abnormalities led to varying sub-types of melancholia and that different personality types were related to the humours, such as sanguine, choleric, melancholic, and phlegmatic temperaments. This is one of the earliest descriptions of the idea that individuals could have a personality style or temperament that may be associated with developing a mental condition. According to Galen, treatments should include blood-letting if the melancholia was thought to be a brain disease sub-type, but bathing, rest, and a well-balanced diet if it had different origins (e.g. the blood or the stomach). Like Rufus, Galen produced a remedy called theriac (a term which is sometimes translated as antidote).

Over the following centuries there was general acceptance of humoral disequilibrium as the cause of melancholia in many cultures. For example, the Arabian physician Avicenna (the Latin version of his name), who is also known as Abu Ali al Husain ibn Abd, wrote about melancholia and the four humours in the highly influential *Canon of Medicine*. In this book, he suggested that both the body and soul were affected by melancholia and advocated the use of persuasive talking as a method of treatment, which some have suggested may have been a forerunner to cognitive behaviour therapy.

In this era, there were further developments in regard to views about the nature of the problem and its treatments. For example, Aretaeus of Cappadocia highlighted the cyclical nature of episodes of melancholia and noted that it may be associated with mania. Similar observations were made by others, such as Alexander of Tralles (AD 525–605), but Aretaeus is regarded as the 'clinician of mania', which he described as a state characterized by furor, excitement, and cheerfulness. Aretaeus proposed that some cases of melancholia might be precipitated by external events such as bereavement, and that love (which he referred to as The Physician Love) could help alleviate the symptoms of melancholia, as could eating blackberries and leeks and talking about symptoms.

In the era this was written, medicine and philosophy occupied parallel worlds with limited cross-fertilization of ideas. Whilst most of the texts by physicians focused on melancholia, there were other observations on human emotions, including dejection and sadness, recorded by the philosophers of the time. For example, Epictetus, a Stoic philosopher of the 1st century AD, wrote that 'Men are disturbed not by things but the views which they take of them.' In modern psychiatry, the Stoics are often quoted in discussions of stress-vulnerability models, as their ideas offer potentially simple insights into why the experience of the same life event, such as loss or the breakup of a relationship, may be followed by an episode of clinical depression in one individual but not in another.

The Middle Ages

From about AD 500 onwards, there was a significant shift away from the notion that mental disorders had similar causes to physical disorders and should be treated by physicians towards a revival of beliefs that mental disorders were signs of immorality, sin, and evil. Christianity dominated the social order and religious doctrines were evident not just in the anti-science of that era and the shifting explanations of the causes of melancholia but also in ideas about what constituted appropriate interventions, which increasingly became the responsibility of the clergy rather than clinicians.

In her book *The Nature of Melancholy*, Jennifer Radden chronicles many classical accounts of these views such as the story of Hildegard of Bingen (1098–1179). Hildegard was a German nun who wrote the *Book of Holistic Healings*, which drew upon humoral theories of melancholia but then proposed that black bile had come to exist because of original sin. Similar views were reported by other influential people of the time and any mental condition characterized by loss of reason was regarded as evidence of God's punishment. As such, melancholia was viewed as a challenge to Christian faith and morals. This inevitably led to the sufferer being demonized and many melancholics were burned at the stake as witches. In 1486, a manual on witch-hunting, the *Malleus Maleficarum* (The Hammer of the Witches), was written for Pope Innocent VIII by a famous inquisitor for the Catholic Church, Heinrich Kramer (see Figure 2). Amazingly, the text was revised and reprinted more than sixteen times over the next 200 years and it remained influential across Europe until the early years of the Renaissance.

It is worth noting that some European groups rejected the notion that mental disorders offered evidence of evil or possession by the devil. For example, the Saturnists believed that melancholia was caused by celestial influences that especially afflicted the most talented and creative members of society, and so melancholia was an experience to be admired. Marsilio Ficino (1433–99) is the person most commonly regarded as a leader of the Saturnists. He was born in Italy and trained in philosophy and medicine and experienced episodes of melancholia himself. Ficino advocated treatments such as exercise, alternative diets, and music. He believed that the horoscope dictated character and he also supported the Aristotelian idea that melancholia was linked with intelligence, which was connected to the planet Saturn.

Historical accounts of the Middle Ages largely focus on the negative and hostile reactions towards people with melancholia from all classes and subgroups within society. However, it is worth highlighting that these attitudes were not universal across all cultures. The emphasis on the ideas expressed in the literature originating in Europe, and then later in the New World, often fail to include the range of views expressed in other cultures and religions (see Box 1). We do not examine these views and attitudes

MALLEVS

MALEFICARVM,

MALEFICAS ET EARVM

hæresim frameâ conterens,

EX VARIIS AVCTORIBVS COMPILATVS,
& in quatuor Tomos iuſtè diſtributus;

QVORVM DVO PRIORES VANAS DÆMONVM
verſutias, præſtigioſas eorum deluſiones, ſuperſtitioſas Strigimagarum
cæremonias, horrendos etiam cum illis congreſſus; exactam denique
tam peſtiferæ ſectæ diſquiſitionem, & punitionem complectuntur.
Tertius praxim Exorciſtarum ad Dæmonum, & Strigimagarum male-
ficia de Chriſti fidelibus pellenda; Quartus verò Artem Doctrinalem,
Benedictionalem, & Exorciſmalem continent.

TOMVS PRIMVS.

Indices Auctorum, capitum, rerúmque non deſunt.

Editio nouiſſima, infinitis penè mendis expurgata; cuique acceſſit Fuga
Dæmonum & Complementum artis exorciſticæ.

Vir ſiue mulier, in quibus Pythonicus, vel diuinationis fuerit ſpiritus, morte moriatur
Leuitici cap. 10.

LVGDVNI,
Sumptibus CLAVDII BOVRGEAT, ſub ſigno Mercurij Galli.

M. DC. LXIX.
CVM PRIVILEGIO REGIS.

2. The cover of *Malleus Maleficarum* (The Hammer of the Witches).

Box 1 Cultural differences in views of melancholia

Islam: The teachings of the prophet Muhammad stated that individuals with mental disorders were dear to their God and should be treated humanely and cared for by society. It was thought that illnesses such as melancholia were a sign of supernatural intervention and that it was important to provide the individual with a calm and restful atmosphere. This probably explains why this culture is regarded as possibly the first to develop asylums.

Ayurveda: The ancient Hindu scriptures of Ramayana and Mahabharata contain descriptions of depression. Ayurveda, an Indian system of medicine, was first described in the 1st and 2nd centuries AD. In Ayurveda there are three bodily humours or doshas: Vata, Pitta, and Kapha. Disturbances of the doshas relative to each other lead to illness (similar to humoral theory). Depression was and still is classified according to which dosha is dominant. Vata depression is characterized by anxiety, guilt, and insomnia and may be caused by upsetting experiences. Pitta depression is shown by irritability, low self-esteem, and suicidality and can be associated with overwork and lack of sunlight. Kapha depression is associated with excessive sleep, overeating, and lethargy and may be caused by lack of stimulation.

Judaism: Ancient Judaism viewed mental illness as possession by demons and was seen as a punishment from God for failure to uphold traditions. Those afflicted were treated well in the main, but law reduced their responsibilities in society.

Traditional Chinese medicine: According to traditional Chinese medicine, depression is caused by a blockage of the internal organs and meridians that connect them and it is proposed that this restrains the flow of Qi (which represents energy) to various organs, which causes stagnation. Suggested treatments included acupuncture, exercise, and the 'mood smooth': a specific mixture of Chinese herbs with some similarities to thearic (an ancient remedy).

in detail, but offer a brief synopsis to raise awareness of these
cultural differences.

From the age of enlightenment to the birth of modern psychiatry

From the 1500s onwards new attitudes towards melancholia
began to emerge. Joan Luis Vives (1492–1540) expressed the idea
that individuals with mental illness should be respected and
treated rather than denigrated by society. Likewise Johann Weyer
(1515–88) stated that individuals should not be punished or
blamed for their 'disordered imaginations' and highlighted the
importance of building a therapeutic relationship between
a patient and a physician; an idea that holds to this day.

Perhaps the best-known text from the Renaissance is *The
Anatomy of Melancholy* or to give it its full title *The Anatomy of
Melancholy, What it is: With all the Kinds, Causes, Symptomes,
Prognostickes, and Several Cures of it. In Three Maine Partitions
with their Several Sections, Members, and Subsections.
Philosophically, Medicinally, Historically, Opened and Cut Up*.
Written by the Oxford academic Robert Burton and first
published in 1621, it offers a somewhat eccentric (the text is
presented in the voice of an imaginary Greek philosopher,
Democritus Junior) but detailed account of all aspects of
melancholia. Although Burton's work is often regarded as a
medical treatise, it is really a historical overview of differing ideas
about melancholy from the perspective of philosophy, psychology,
physiology, demonology, cosmology, meteorology, etc. Despite all
its flaws, the book remains the most widely quoted historical
account of different types of melancholy, the proposed physical
and psychological causes, and various potential cures including
prayer, healthy living, entertainment, talking with friends, and
ancient remedies such as purgation. Interestingly, Burton also
made one of the first known references to treatment with St John's
Wort ('if gathered on a Friday night in the hour of Jupiter'), which

has been proposed as a modern-day natural remedy for depression.

Another great chronicler of the 17th-century period was Richard Napier, an English physician and clergyman. He recorded observations on over 2,000 mentally ill patients and believed that 20 per cent of these patients had some form of melancholia. Napier subscribed to the view that the term melancholia should be reserved for individuals from higher social classes. He suggested that poorer patients with similar clinical problems were described as being 'mopish', which was a lower status and more stigmatizing diagnosis. Napier's social classification of the disorder suggests he was influenced by assumptions that true melancholia was associated with moral superiority and intellectual prowess. Indeed, during this era melancholia became a sought after disposition or diagnosis by some.

Thomas Willis (1621–75) is another important figure from this era, and he is remembered as one of the first proponents of chemical as opposed to humoral theories of the causes of melancholia. He identified the weather, excessive thinking, and insufficient exercise as causes of chemical disruptions in the body and advocated treatments such as spa waters containing iron. The rise of chemical theories signalled the demise of humoral theories. However, studies of the human body were evolving rapidly and new understandings of the circulatory systems, such as described by the English physician William Harvey, meant that chemical theories were soon surpassed by the so-called mechanical theories of physical and mental illnesses.

Mechanical theories of melancholia suggested that it developed when the flow of blood, lymph, and animal spirits in the body was slowed down or stagnated. Freidrich Hoffman (1660–1742) suggested this was due to disequilibrium of different types of fluids whilst others, such as the Dutch physician Herman Boerhaave (1668–1738), cited thickening of the blood with 'oily and fatty stuffs'. By contrast, William Cullen (1710–90) focused attention on the nervous system and proposed that melancholia resulted when there was disturbed nerve fluid flow and reduced excitability in the nervous system.

At about the same time as these developments in the theories about the causes of melancholia a number of clinicians began to report that melancholia was a problem that tended to be recurrent and that it could be linked to mania. For example, a Spanish physician named Andrés Piquer-Arrufat diagnosed King Ferdinand VI with 'affectivo melancholico maniaca'. Interestingly, his contribution is often overlooked as two French psychiatrists described a similar disorder within weeks of each other in 1854 (but 100 years later than Piquer-Arrufat). Jules Baillarger called it 'la folie a double form' (dual form madness) whilst Jean Pierre Falret named it 'la folie circulaire' (circular madness) and recorded 'this succession of mania and melancholia manifests itself with continuity and in a manner almost regular'.

The 18th century also heralded a change in the way patients were viewed and treated. One of the best-known reformers was Philippe Pinel, a French psychiatrist trained in literature, religion, mathematics, and medicine. In his text *Traité médico-philosophique sur l'aliénation mentale*, he categorized mental disorders into mania, melancholia, dementia, and idiotism. Pinel recognized that mania (that often presented with exalted self-importance and pretensions of unbounded power) and melancholia (that often presented with depression of the spirits, apprehensions, and absolute despair) were different expressions of the same disorder. An idea that was reinforced by others, such as Esquirol during the following century. Pinel also contributed to the developing dialogue about the potential causes of these disorders. For example, he suggested that melancholia could occur as a consequence of domestic misfortunes, obstacles to marriage, and disappointed ambition. He also observed that it occurred as a result of a combination of the makeup of the person and the meaning of the stress they experienced; ideas that echo those of the Stoic philosophers.

In the USA, Benjamin Rush (1745–1813), who is often described as the Father of American Psychiatry, was working as a physician in Philadelphia and began to develop his own rather complex theory about melancholia. He coined the term tristimania for a less severe form and amenomania for a more severe form of illness. Rush proposed that a reaction in the blood vessels of the brain (convulsive motions that he termed 'morbid excitement') caused these symptoms and believed that spinning the patient would reduce the inflammation, and devised a tranquilizing chair. Although this particular treatment was both unpleasant and ineffective, Rush remains a well-regarded clinician and renowned as a social activist who advocated free treatment for the poor.

The late 18th and early 19th centuries saw an ongoing debate about biological or psychological causes of melancholia. Psychological models still retained religious or moral overtones. For example, Johann Christain Heinroth (1773–1843), a member of the German Psychiker School (literally meaning psychologically orientated school), viewed the sins of the patient as the root of their mental illness. In contrast, Wilheim Greisinger (1817–68) stated that 'mental diseases are somatic diseases of the brain'. He suggested that each disorder represented a stage of a single brain disorder, a concept termed 'Einheitspsychose' (the unitary psychosis). In 1845 he published *Pathology and Therapy of the Nervous Diseases* which emphasized his view that psychiatry was a medical scientific specialty. Greisinger's views on psychosis and psychiatry were influential in Germany and beyond and led to a debate that continues to this day.

We conclude this chapter with a man whose name lives on into the modern times because a famous psychiatric institution, the Maudsley Hospital, is named after him. Henry Maudsley (1835–1918) suggested that insanity could be divided into affective and ideational categories. This represents an important idea as it begins the process of separating disorders associated with mood disturbances from mental disorders that were characterized by delusions (psychotic disorders); he also believed that there was a physical cause for mental disorders. In many ways Maudsley provides a bridge between the ancient and the modern era and he was practising psychiatry at around the time that the term depression was being used more frequently, with the word melancholia increasingly reserved for the most severe forms of the illness. This was the start of an era in which medical theories about melancholia began to be integrated with ideas about sadness and dejection described by philosophers, psychologists, and also by Freud.

Chapter 2
The modern era: Diagnosis and classification of depression

Early observations of melancholia (the most severe form of depression) suggested that it could have physical or psychological origins and that depression and mania could occur at different times in the same person. Although theories about the underlying causes of depression changed over the centuries, there was a remarkable level of consistency in the descriptions of the core symptoms with sadness and despondency accompanied by sleep problems and physical complaints. However, mental illness remained a broad concept in the 18th and 19th centuries and whilst evidence of 'madness' frequently led to admission to an asylum, there were only rudimentary attempts to differentiate between or classify mental disorders.

The turn of the 20th century saw huge changes. There was a realization that severe mental illnesses (increasingly referred to as psychosis) were not uniform and that this 'loss of reason' might take different forms. Also, less severe but disabling forms of mental disorder (sometimes called neuroses) were described and there was a move towards providing private outpatient treatments for many of these individuals. To give an insight into these developments and how they influenced current thinking on depression, we briefly review the contributions of Emil Kraepelin and Sigmund Freud. The ideas expressed by these two individuals have moved in and out of fashion over the last century. We include these descriptions because, whether current experts, clinicians, or readers of this text agree or disagree with the views put forward by Kraepelin or Freud, it is clear that their theories have cast a long shadow over our understanding of depression and its treatment.

Kraepelin and the classification of psychoses

Emil Kraepelin was, and remains, one of the most influential figures in psychiatry. He was born in 1856 in Neustrelitz in north Germany. After qualifying in medicine he trained in psychiatry in Munich where the emphasis was to find a physical cause of mental illness through studying the brain. Kraepelin was also interested in other approaches and models, and he worked in Leipzig with Wilhelm Wundt, a well-known psychologist. Kraepelin worked as an asylum psychiatrist, became a professor, and then moved to Heidelberg where he began his now famous meticulous studies of asylum patients. He kept written cards on each patient noting their symptoms and the course and outcome of their illness and then wrote a series of textbooks (entitled *Psychiatrie*) where he described his observations of clinical cases and emerging ideas on how to categorize mental conditions. Kraepelin highlighted that the causes of psychiatric illnesses were largely not understood, and that the same mental symptoms could occur in more than one disorder, but he suggested that the course and outcome of the clinical presentation could be used to distinguish between subgroups of patients with different diagnoses. In 1899, Kraepelin described the identification of two distinct types of 'functional' (non-organic) psychotic illness: Manic Depressive Insanity and Dementia Praecox (which we now know as schizophrenia).

In Kraepelin's classification, Dementia Praecox included all psychotic illnesses without an overt mood component, and these patients showed gradual continuous decline without any periods of recovery; Kraepelin believed that this presentation eventually progressed to dementia. In contrast, those with Manic Depressive Insanity usually (but not always) demonstrated changes in mood, cognition, and behaviour (referred to as motor activity). Also, these changes followed an intermittent and recurrent course, with periods of recovery between episodes. He stated that the term Manic Depressive Insanity described a number of related mood disorders and that 'as its name indicates, it takes its course in single attacks, which either present the signs of so called manic excitement (flight of ideas, exaltation and over-activity), or those of a peculiar psychic depression with psychomotor inhibition, or a mixture of the two states'.

Kraepelin regarded melancholia as part of the spectrum of Manic Depressive Insanity and noted that the treatment of the former often overlapped with the treatment of the latter. He also believed that his classification system would ultimately be validated by medical research that would identify the underlying causes of the illnesses.

The recognition of the two conditions (Dementia Praecox and Manic Depressive Insanity) was not entirely new, but Kraepelin offered the clearest and most decisive descriptions. Nevertheless, his proposed classification was not universally accepted, and even today there is considerable debate about how he categorized certain mood disorders or personality problems, including conditions such as chronic depression. Kraepelin's attempts to develop a more systematic framework for defining different patterns of illness and disease progression still influence modern classification systems for mental disorders to this day, although the term manic depressive illness has largely been replaced by the term bipolar disorder (see Box 2).

Box 2 Manic depression or bipolar disorder

Kraepelin classified all mood disorders as part of the spectrum of manic depressive insanity.

Over time, an alternative model began to be accepted which hypothesized that there were two distinct categories of mood disorder: one where patients experience episodes of mania and depression and another where depression only is experienced. In 1957 Karl Leonhard, a German psychiatrist, is credited with coining the term 'bipolar' to describe the condition of episodic mania and depression and 'unipolar' for illness characterized by depression only. These terms may have been used by his predecessor Karl Kleist; a German psychiatrist with whom Leonhard worked.

This distinction between unipolar and bipolar disorders was further validated in 1966 by Perris and Angst who found that the two conditions could be distinguished by differences in family history of the disorder. In the 1960s, the term bipolar disorder was used for the first time to replace manic depression in the published diagnostic manuals.

Freud and the classification of neuroses

Sigmund Freud was born in 1856 in Freiburg, a small town in Moravia. He was the eldest of eight children and it is said that he was his mother's favourite. Indeed, many texts on the early life of Freud make much of the fact that his mother called him 'my golden Sigi'. The family moved to Vienna when Freud was young and he remained there until 1938 when he moved to London to escape the persecution of Jews at the outbreak of the Second World War.

Freud became interested in neurology when he was a medical student and in 1885 he went to study with the famous neurologist Jean-Martin Charcot at the Salpêtrière Institute in Paris. Charcot had an interest in hysteria, which was described as a neurotic condition because physical symptoms experienced by the patient such as paralysis did not have a clear physical (organic) basis. Charcot used hypnosis to demonstrate that the patient's clinical presentation was associated with ongoing conflicts that could explain the symptoms experienced, and argued that the patient's psychological distress had been transformed or 'converted' into a physical problem. Charcot proposed that the use of hypnotic suggestion could release these unconscious forces and bring about improvement.

Freud realized that the unconscious mind had a very powerful effect upon behaviour, and extended the use of hypnosis to uncover unconscious memories of traumas which the person was not aware of and had repressed. Through a series of detailed case studies, Freud developed theories to explain how unresolved conflicts from the past could produce specific neurotic symptoms and illness later in life. He then proposed that psychoanalysis could help resolve these conflicts and create a healthier mental state.

Freud's concepts of depression can be traced to his three hypothetical models of how the mind (or psyche as he called it) is organized, how personality develops, and the possible causes of neurotic illness. These models are reviewed very briefly to give a flavour of the ideas expressed, but interested readers may wish to consult other texts to examine these ideas in detail. In his first theory, called the topography of the mind, Freud suggested that the mind had three parts: the conscious, the preconscious (things we are not currently attending to, but that we can access and focus on), and the unconscious (which we are unaware of, but which can exert influence upon us).

Freud also described a structural model of how personality shapes our actions and reactions, a theory that is sometimes called the second topography. This is important because it introduced the concepts of the id, ego, and superego. In Freud's view, the id is driven by the pleasure principle, namely a need for the immediate gratification of its desires and functions in the unconscious. The ego strives to satisfy the id in appropriate ways, operating as an intermediary between the id and the outside world. The ego is associated with the reality principle, for example allowing delayed gratification of the id to occur in a socially acceptable manner and at an appropriate moment in time. Freud proposed a range of defence mechanisms that were used to maintain equilibrium including, for example, rationalizing the reasons for acting in a certain way or being in denial about the consequences of an impulsive behaviour. The superego is the final element of personality that develops (around the age of 5 years) and it provides a sense of right and wrong and modifies the actions of the ego. For healthy personality development Freud suggested that the id, the ego, and the superego have to be in balance. He believed that any imbalance would lead to the development of a neurosis such as depression or anxiety. For example, Freud suggested that if the drives of the id override the superego, guilt is experienced, or if the ego suppresses the id, anxiety occurs.

Freud's third theory of the mind concerned childhood sexual development and the stages that an infant has to pass through successfully to become a healthy adult. The theory divides human development into a predictable sequence such as the oral, anal, and phallic stages (associated with the Oedipus complex), etc. Freud believed conflict in any of the stages explained both the later development of neurosis and the type of symptoms experienced. He also proposed certain personality traits were associated with failure to pass through a specific stage of development. For example, Freud proposed that difficulties in the anal stage were related to the development of obsessional symptoms. In contrast, difficulties in the oral stage were manifest in adult life by personality traits such as passivity, dependency, and self-doubt which he suggested were common in people prone to developing depression.

In 1917, Freud published a famous work entitled *Mourning and Melancholia* in which he compared melancholia (severe depression) with mourning (the grief experienced by someone following a bereavement). He described both conditions as being associated with loss but suggested that the difference was in the feelings associated with the different types of loss. In mourning the loss was recognized at a conscious level—the person who has died was the 'lost object' and the feelings associated with the bereavement such as sadness and anger were expressed outwardly. In contrast, Freud proposed that in melancholia the loss was of an 'ideal object', for example the loss of love (e.g. experienced after rejection or the breakdown of a relationship). Furthermore, he suggested that, unlike mourning, the loss was partly unconscious in melancholia and anger towards the lost object was redirected against the self. In addition, Freud stated that a person who reacts to loss by developing melancholia has either reverted to, or never moved on from, an earlier stage of development. He stated that those who are likely to become depressed have an impaired sense of self-worth so when the 'object' is lost they have nothing to fall back on of themselves and this lack of resilience increases the risk that they will become depressed.

Freud differentiated depression from other neuroses on the basis of symptoms and the hypothesized development origins. Nowadays, many of his ideas have been discarded or revised, but his work helped to illuminate the continuum from 'normal sadness' to depression and how personality characteristics and illness symptoms can overlap. However, Freud's models arose from work undertaken mainly with upper- or middle-class women in a private outpatient clinic in Vienna—a very different population from the asylum cases observed by Kraepelin that informed the categorization of psychoses. Nevertheless, the ideas of both men influenced later attempts to define the boundaries of depression and approaches to diagnosis and classification of mental disorders.

Boundary: a dividing line, a line that marks the limit of an area

One of the problems encountered in any discussion of depression is that the word is used to mean different things by different people. For many members of the public, the term depression is used to describe normal sadness. In clinical practice, the term depression can be used to describe negative mood states, which are symptoms that can occur in a range of illnesses (e.g. individuals with psychosis may also report depressed mood). However, the term depression can also be used to refer to a diagnosis. When employed in this way it is meant to indicate that a cluster of symptoms have all occurred together, with the most common changes being in mood, thoughts, feelings, and behaviours. Theoretically, all these symptoms need to be present to make a diagnosis of depressive disorder.

The word diagnosis originates from Greek, from 'dia' apart and 'gignokein' to recognize or know. In any medical speciality, the first step in making a diagnosis is an assessment interview. In branches of medicine other than psychiatry a range of investigations can be used to aid the process of diagnosis. For example, a suspected diagnosis of ischaemic heart disease can be confirmed by performing an angiogram (a test in which a special dye is injected into the blood vessels that can make visible any narrowing of the arteries supplying blood to the heart muscles). The absence of any laboratory tests in psychiatry means that the diagnosis of depression relies on clinical judgement and the recognition of patterns of symptoms. There are two main problems with this. First, the diagnosis represents an attempt to impose a 'present/absent' or 'yes/no' classification on a problem that, in reality, is dimensional and varies in duration and severity. Also, many symptoms are likely to show some degree of overlap with pre-existing personality traits.

Taken together, this means there is an ongoing concern about the point at which depression or depressive symptoms should be regarded as a mental disorder, that is, where to situate the dividing line on a continuum from health to normal sadness to illness. Second, for many years, there was a lack of consistent agreement on what combination of symptoms and impaired functioning would benefit from clinical intervention. This lack of consensus on the threshold for treatment, or for deciding which treatment to use, is a major source of problems to this day.

Such issues have undermined research in mood disorders, clinical practice, and also public confidence in the concept of depression and rationale for its treatment. Over a number of decades, there have been international efforts to standardize approaches to diagnosis through the introduction of criterion-based classifications of mental disorders. Box 3 gives an example of the criteria used for the diagnosis of major depression according to the *Diagnostic and Statistical Manual of Mental Disorders (IVth Edition)* of the American Psychiatric Association (this set of criteria is not the most recent, but was chosen as they are easier to digest than some of the others). The process of applying these criteria goes through several steps. For example, if it is determined that the symptoms a person

---

Box 3 An example of diagnostic criteria for major depression

A. Five (or more) of the following symptoms have been present during the same two-week period and represent a change from previous functioning; at least one of the symptoms is either (1) depressed mood or (2) loss of interest or pleasure.

    (1) depressed mood most of the day, nearly every day, as indicated by subjective or observer reports

    (2) markedly diminished interest or pleasure in all, or almost all, activities most of the day, nearly every day

(3) significant weight loss when not dieting or weight gain, or decrease or increase in appetite nearly every day

(4) insomnia or hypersomnia nearly every day

(5) psychomotor agitation or retardation nearly every day (observable by others, not merely subjective feelings of restlessness or being slowed down)

(6) fatigue or loss of energy nearly every day

(7) feelings of worthlessness or excessive or inappropriate guilt nearly every day

(8) diminished ability to think or concentrate, or indecisiveness, nearly every day

(9) recurrent thoughts of death (not just fear of dying), recurrent suicidal ideation without a specific plan, or a suicide attempt or a specific plan for committing suicide.

B. The symptoms do not meet criteria for a Mixed Episode (co-occurrence of depression and mania).

C. The symptoms cause clinically significant distress or impairment in social, occupational, or other important areas of functioning.

D. The symptoms are not due to the direct physiological effects of a substance (e.g. abuse of a drug, the effects of a medication) or a general medical condition (e.g. hypothyroidism).

E. The symptoms are not better accounted for by Bereavement. (Interestingly, this criterion is excluded from the new version of the classification system.)

reports can be categorized as a depressive disorder, a dimensional rating of the intensity of the symptoms is then made to clarify if the depression should be regarded as mild, moderate, or severe. Other steps are also possible. For example, it is possible to specify additional features of the presentation such as whether the depression is accompanied by any loss of reality (psychotic depression), etc.

A careful inspection of the criteria for identifying a depressive disorder demonstrates that diagnosis is mainly reliant on the cross-sectional assessment of the way the person presents at that moment in time. It is also emphasized that the current presentation should represent a change from the person's usual state, as this step helps to begin the process of differentiating illness episodes from long-standing personality traits. Clarifying the longitudinal history of any lifetime problems can help also to establish, for example, whether the person has previously experienced mania (in which case their diagnosis will be revised to bipolar disorder), or whether they have a history of chronic depression, with persistent symptoms that may be less severe but are nevertheless very debilitating (this is usually called dysthymia). In addition, it is important to assess whether the person has another mental or physical disorder as well as these may frequently co-occur with depression.

The classification systems introduced for mental disorders were initially developed separately in America (Diagnostic and Statistical Manual of Mental Disorders or DSM) and Europe (International Classification of Diseases or ICD). However, attempts have been made with the most recent revisions of these classification systems to more closely match the diagnostic approaches, to improve international consistency, and ensure groups are communicating about and comparing the same problem. In the absence of diagnostic tests, the current classifications still rely on expert consensus regarding symptom profiles.

The classification system is not static and the range of presentations of depression that are recognized and their location within the classification manuals has changed over time. For example, in the early editions of DSM (which were influenced by Freud's models of depression), persistent but milder depressive symptoms (referred to as dysthymia) were regarded primarily as a personality type and so they were located within that category in the textbook on classification. Later revisions of DSM were based less on unproven theoretical models, and tried to make decisions about classification based on empirical evidence. Several research studies indicated there were many overlaps between major depressive and dysthymic symptoms, and that 80 per cent of individuals with dysthymia experience a major depression at some point in their life. As such, it was argued that dysthymia should be reclassified as a type of mood disorder.

Moving the location of a condition within a classification system may seem like an academic or intellectual exercise, but it is important to recognize that such shifts can have significant implications as one of the roles of diagnosis and classification is to guide treatment decisions. The relocation of dysthymia meant that the treatments offered shifted from psychotherapy only (an intervention recommended to address difficulties experienced as a consequence of certain personality traits) to options that included both therapy and medications (as used for many mood disorders). However, this simple example exposes the weaknesses of the current system. Even if changes to the classification system can be justified on the basis of new scientific findings, they are potentially open to biases and so it is all too obvious why it provokes scepticism in some quarters.

In summary, for a classification system to have utility it needs to be reliable and valid. If a diagnosis is reliable doctors will all make the same diagnosis when they interview patients who present with the same set of symptoms. If a diagnosis has predictive validity it means that it is possible to forecast the future course of the illness in individuals with the same diagnosis and to anticipate their likely response to different treatments. For many decades, the lack of reliability so undermined the credibility of psychiatric diagnoses that most of the revisions of the classification systems between the 1950s and 2010 focused on improving diagnostic reliability. However, insufficient attention has been given to validity and until this is improved, the criteria used for diagnosing depressive disorders will continue to be regarded as somewhat arbitrary (e.g. there is little empirical evidence to support the use of a cut-off of the presence of a minimum five out of nine symptoms persisting for two weeks for diagnosing a depression as a major episode).

Weaknesses in the systems for the diagnosis and classification of depression are frequently raised in discussions about the existence of depression as a separate entity and concerns about the rationale for treatment. It is notable that general medicine uses a similar approach to making decisions regarding the health–illness dimension. For example, levels of blood pressure exist on a continuum. However, when an individual's blood pressure measurement reaches a predefined level, it is reported that the person now meets the criteria specified for the diagnosis of hypertension (high blood pressure). Depending on the degree of variation from the norm or average values for their age and gender, the person will be offered different interventions. They may be asked to attend regular monitoring sessions and to modify their lifestyle. However, if the problem persists or is regarded as more severe, a range of other interventions and treatment with medications may be suggested. This approach is widely accepted as a rational approach to managing this common physical health problem, yet a similar 'stepped care' approach to depression is often derided. This exposes the frequent double standards that seem to operate for common physical health as compared to mental health problems, where the same approach to clinical management is regarded as unscientific or controversial for depression.

It is worth noting that, in the absence of objective laboratory tests, the current approach to the diagnosis of depression does have the benefit of pragmatism. It can be argued that when the severity, duration, degree of distress, and level of social impairment associated with a set of symptoms reach an agreed threshold then the problem warrants clinical attention and the individual deserves help to cope with these experiences.

Chapter 3
Who is at risk of depression?

One advantage of the more consistent application of diagnostic
criteria for identifying individuals with a depressive disorder is
that it allows national and international comparisons to be
undertaken. Large-scale studies make it possible to estimate the
overall prevalence of depression, and repeating the surveys allows
detection of any changes in these rates over time. Comparisons
can be made between the distribution of depression cases by
country, culture, economic and social status, and other demographic
features such as age, gender, marital status, etc. Differences between
any of these subgroups can offer important insights into who is at
risk of depression, at what time point an episode is most likely to
occur, and also the development of theories about what factors
reduce the risk of or protect against such experiences.

We explore the epidemiology of depression (which refers to the
distribution and determinants of depression-related states), give
examples of the presentation of depression across the lifespan,
and discuss some gender-related issues. Lastly, we highlight some
of the current thinking on the prevention of suicide.

Epidemiology

The World Health Organization (WHO) has estimated that over
5 per cent of the global population will be depressed during any

one year and that about 15 per cent of the population will experience a depression at some point during their lifetime. On average an episode will last between four and eight months, but recurrences are common and about 50 per cent of depression cases will have at least one further episode of depression within five years. Lamentably, the WHO also reports that only 25 per cent of those who experience a depressive episode will have access to effective treatments. However, behind these headline figures there is considerable variation in the estimated rates—so here are a few examples that have been chosen simply to illustrate some of these differences. We emphasize that the list of issues we discuss is not exhaustive, but the topics have been selected to show how researchers use these data to begin to develop theories about why certain sub-populations are more or less likely to become depressed.

Geography

The prevalence of depression is not uniform across countries or continents. For example, rates are reported to be especially high in France and America. The reasons for this are unclear; there are similarly high rates in India, whilst some of the lowest rates are reported in Taiwan and China. There is some suggestion that it is not geography but Gross Domestic Product (GDP) that may in part explain these different rates—with depression being more common in high-income countries (about 15 per cent) compared to low- to middle-income countries (just over 10 per cent).

There has long been a suggestion (first put forward by researchers in schizophrenia) that agrarian societies may be less stressful places to live than industrialized or urban environments and also that such communities may be more tolerant and supportive of individuals with depression. It is unclear if this can explain the geographical variations in depression rates, but the data from countries such as India are interesting given that it is a continent that is undergoing significant social and economic changes. It is proposed that transitional regions may show greater instability because the conflict in values between metropolitan and more rural settings potentially increases stress levels in these areas. The theory suggests that individuals who are vulnerable to depression are therefore more likely to experience an illness episode than similar individuals living in more stable regions. In contrast it is argued that the lower rates of depression reported in some countries (such as China) could be explained by the fact that some individuals or social groups are still less likely to recognize, acknowledge, or seek help for psychological problems.

Culture and ethnicity

Depression and its symptoms may be expressed differently in different ethnic groups and cultures. A simple example of this phenomenon comes from one of the recent large-scale community studies undertaken in America that was published in 2012. The one-year prevalence of depression was virtually the same in Hispanic and White Americans (about 7 per cent), slightly lower in Black Americans (just over 6 per cent), about 3 per cent in Asian Americans, but about 10 per cent in Alaskan natives. It is possible that the reported rates are influenced by the nature of how depression is perceived by the individual. It is known that in some cultures or ethnic groups more attention is given to physical experiences (such as low energy, poor appetite, and disturbed sleep) rather than to psychological or emotional symptoms of depression. For example, individuals from Asian countries or cultures are more likely to report physical symptoms. So, it is possible that publications that indicate low rates of depression are underestimating the actual rates. Alternatively, it could be that the different rates are not due to differences in reporting of symptoms, but that there may be specific risk or protective factors operating within these different ethnic groups or cultures that modify the level of risk for developing depression in different sub-populations in the USA.

Socio-economics

A 2010 survey comparing rates of depression in Germany, America, and England found that depression was most prevalent in the poorest sub-sample of respondents (18–27 per cent) and lowest in the wealthiest sub-sample (4–10 per cent). Other research indicates that rates of depression are about three times higher in those who are unemployed as compared to those who are employed. These data are often viewed as controversial, mainly because they are interpreted (used and misused) in different ways by different political groups. However, it must be recognized that evidence of increased prevalence rates does not in itself explain the direction of causality, that is, we cannot assume that unemployment increases the likelihood of depression, as it is possible that the depression came first and reduced a person's ability to gain or maintain employment, with knock-on effects for income levels and quality of life. Indeed, in this example, the relationship may well be bidirectional, with unemployment increasing the risk of depression and depression increasing the risk that someone will be unemployed.

Chronology

In international studies the average age of onset of the first episode of depression is the mid-to-late twenties; and it has been reported that the first experience occurs about two years earlier in lower- as compared to higher-income countries. In large-scale community studies undertaken in America, the one-year rate of depression was higher in 18–25-year-olds (around one in ten) than in any other age group. Worldwide, about 40 per cent of people report the initial episode of depression occurred before the age of 20 years, about 50 per cent report it began between 20 and 50 years, whilst only 10 per cent state their first experience of depression occurred after the age of 50 years.

Interestingly, there is evidence that the rates of depression and age of onset have changed over the last fifty to sixty years and that the risk of experiencing at least one episode of depression has increased and the age of onset of the first episode has decreased in individuals born after the Second World War. Suggested reasons for these temporal changes vary from the notion that the increase in reported rates of depression offers evidence of medicalization, that is, that normal sadness is being misdiagnosed as illness. Other suggested explanations are that the increase in rates of depression is an artefact of increased access to health services for all members of society (i.e. depression rates are unchanged, but detection has increased) or that more people are prepared to seek help.

If medicalization or changes in treatment seeking do not explain the observed changes in rates of depression and age of onset of the first episode, it is interesting to consider other reasons. The relatively short time frame during which this increase has occurred means it is unlikely to be explained by genetics as changes in our genetic makeup only become apparent after many hundreds of years. However, social and environmental changes can have an impact within a few decades on our health and well-being. For example, research suggests that increased exposure to drugs and alcohol in the post-war years may partly explain the increase in depression.

Gender

Rates of depression in women are consistently reported to be twice those reported in men. As this gender gap is found in surveys of both untreated as well as treated populations, it cannot be solely attributable to a greater tendency to recognize, report, or seek treatment for distress in women. Other explanations have been put forward, ranging from the influence of hormones to social role differences, and will be discussed in Chapter 4.

Marital status

Cross-culturally, the loss of a partner, whether by death, divorce, or separation, is associated with increased rates of depression.

Married men have the lowest rates of depression and separated or divorced men have higher rates. There is a less clear association in women. Many explanations for these findings have been proposed, but the answer is not straightforward. For example, it is uncertain whether having depression causes a marriage to fail or if the stress of divorce or separation (or the reason for it) is the cause of depression. Alternatively, another independent factor such as abnormal personality could increase the likelihood someone will become depressed and also interfere with their ability to maintain a long-term relationship.

Depression across the lifespan

In the remainder of this chapter we explore depression in childhood and adolescence, depression in women of childbearing age, and depression in men and co-occurring with physical health problems. Then we highlight issues related to suicide (which is commonest in younger and older adults).

Childhood

For many years, depression was regarded as a disorder of middle-aged and older adults, and children and adolescents were thought to be immune to such experiences. Furthermore, the few dissenting voices who suggested that depressive disorders could have an onset in childhood had little evidence to draw on as participation in research was usually restricted to individuals aged over 18 years. From about 1975 onwards, a number of mental health research institutions began to question the perceived wisdom that childhood depression did not exist and several sophisticated long-term follow-up studies were commenced in which children and adolescents were assessed on several occasions over a number of years to examine how many children became depressed and how many of this group experienced repeated episodes of depression, developed manic depression or other mental health problems, and how many had a single depressive episode without any further mental health problems. In reality, the most important findings from these studies extend beyond simple number crunching, as they offer some important insights into risk and protective factors and the differences in the patterns of depression seen in boys and girls before and after puberty.

In children under the age of 11 years, depression is relatively uncommon. In these pre-pubertal children, there is no evidence of the female predominance that is seen consistently in all other age groups; indeed some studies suggest that the prevalence of depression in young boys may actually be higher than in girls. Interestingly, depression in many children does not occur in isolation and the symptoms are often mixed up with anxiety or irritability. Furthermore, depression is not usually the first problem that the child experiences. In about four out of five young children, the development of depression is a complication of other difficulties such as autism or disruptive behaviour problems. Some researchers speculate that the symptoms of depression observed in these children (such as low energy and altered sleep) may represent an 'exhaustion syndrome' that arises as a consequence of the high level of stress associated with their other problems. This idea is important as it overlaps with theories about the role of an overactive stress hormone system in causing depressive symptoms (see Chapter 4). Another noteworthy finding from these large-scale studies is that children who have a family history of depression (e.g. a parent or grandparent who has been treated for depression) are four times more likely than other children to experience an episode of depression early in their life, and if they have one episode, they are more likely than other children to have further episodes.

Given the scepticism in some quarters about whether depression in adults is a 'manufactured' condition, the reports of depression in children aged 5–11 years have opened a whole new can of worms, not least because of the implications for treatment interventions. Many clinicians are understandably reticent about prescribing medications developed for adult disorders to younger people. Studies suggest that talking therapies such as cognitive behaviour therapy and family approaches can be useful, but recent efforts have also turned to the notion that it is important to try to reduce the likelihood of developing depression by increasing resilience in larger groups of young children who may be at risk. For example, this has led to the exploration of any benefits of including mental health promotion within the school curriculum and the introduction of social-emotional learning (SEL) classes. More specific depression prevention strategies have included projects that offer training in mindfulness for children.

Adolescence

Anyone who has spent more than a few days in the company of an adolescent will be aware that mood states, sleep patterns, and self-esteem are highly variable and transient, but also that intense distress can be quite common. As such, there is a considerable challenge in being certain about when normal adolescent unhappiness evolves into a clinical depressive episode that warrants treatment interventions. That said, some of the most recent research indicates that the prevalence of depression in adolescents is the same as in older adults.

One of the important insights from depression research in adolescents is that it is not chronological age but puberty that seems to herald a sharp surge in reported rates of illness. This suggests that hormonal changes may be important, a hypothesis supported by findings that rates of depression in the post-pubertal period are twice as common in young women as young men. As noted in younger children, those adolescents with a family history of either depression or manic depression have a greater risk of developing depression in early adulthood than those without any family history and a family history is more often found in those who develop recurrent episodes of mood problems.

There are many life events that are experienced by young people that are developmentally normal, but that may still trigger episodes of depression. Issues with peer groups, relationship breakdowns, coping with leaving home, and exposure to drugs and alcohol can all precipitate the onset of episodes of depression especially in individuals who may be more vulnerable to depression for other reasons (such as a family history of mood disorders). Also academic performance and economic issues can play a part in this age group. For example, young people who are not in employment, education, or training (so-called NEETs) report depression rates that are three to five times higher than their non-NEET peers. Whilst it is hard to disentangle cause and effect, this finding serves to demonstrate that any interventions for depression in adolescents and young adults cannot be limited to treating depressive symptoms and may well need to include help with re-engagement with social and academic networks.

Unsurprisingly, adolescents frequently show ambivalence about taking medications for depression. Furthermore, young men do not always find it easy to engage with other available treatment interventions such as talking therapies. Some of the solutions proposed to resolve this dilemma include the use of activity- and behaviour-orientated groups to help tackle the symptoms of depression and the exploration of how to use electronic media such as internet applications or web-based programmes. In countries such as Australia research is being undertaken where these options are offered to all school pupils in a particular academic year (e.g. those taking final school examinations that determine their prospects for entry into higher education). Pupils in these school years are targeted on the basis that the rates of depression can be predicted to rise in the face of such stressors and that prevention may be better than cure.

Many young people who do go through a period of depression will find that such psychological problems are confined to adolescence. However, for others it heralds the start of a condition that can affect them for many years. Trying to identify young people who are most likely to develop recurrent mood episodes is a major research priority. Furthermore, it is important to try to differentiate between individuals who may experience repeated episodes of depression and those who may develop manic as well as depressive episodes. There are only a few clues so far. For example, we now know that 70 per cent of individuals who go on to develop bipolar disorder (or manic depression) in early adulthood report that they had a depressive episode in adolescence. Also, this episode often occurs at a slightly earlier age compared to those who get recurrent depression. However, identifying those young adults with a history of depression who may also be at risk of mania is a considerable challenge, as behaviours that can be part of a manic presentation such as risk taking, disinhibited behaviour, staying up all night, and being the life and soul of a party are not necessarily symptoms of illness in late adolescence.

Currently, having a family history of bipolar disorder is one of the few factors that may identify which young people are more likely to experience mania in the future. The limited ability to predict future bipolar disorder with any certainty is a significant barrier to effective treatment. Several surveys of individuals with bipolar disorder identify that the delay in identifying the problem and offering the most appropriate interventions is one of the biggest issues for patients and their families.

A further issue in trying to identify which individuals will ultimately develop bipolar disorder is that even someone with an above average risk is less likely rather than more likely to ever experience an episode of mania. It is currently estimated that less than one in three individuals with multiple risk factors will develop a full-blown bipolar disorder. As such, it is not rational to start prescribing treatments that are used routinely for older adults with an established illness to individuals at risk of, but who do not have a diagnosis of, bipolar disorder. Some researchers have focused on developing interventions with a high benefit to risk ratio. These include non-medical approaches such as lifestyle management and psycho-education programmes that can help a young person to manage any fledgling symptoms or cope with social problems without the risk of side effects or adverse effects that might be seen with some medications. However, there is not yet sufficient evidence to support the introduction of these strategies in day-to-day clinical practice.

Depression in women of child-bearing age

Rather than considering all manifestations of depression in women, we discuss two depressive disorders associated with child bearing, namely post-natal depression and puerperal psychosis.

The birth of a baby is often a reason for celebration and a post-natal depression associated with such an event is frequently regarded as inexplicable by those outside the immediate family circle. It is easy for people to accept that a new mother may feel emotional or weepy in the days immediately after delivery of a baby, when hormone levels come crashing down, physical exhaustion kicks in, or both parents feel overwhelmed by the responsibility of caring for a new baby. However, these transient 'baby blues' are not the same as a more intense and persistent depressive episode which needs to be viewed as a very serious problem that requires early intervention. Any treatment offered must also address directly the feelings of guilt that are expressed by the mother about becoming depressed.

In most ways, the signs and symptoms of post-natal depression reflect those seen in depressions that occur at other times, but what sets post-natal depression apart is the potential impact on the baby. Not only does the depression impair the mother's self-care and her quality of life, but it may affect the day-to-day care of the baby. Importantly, it can complicate plans for breastfeeding as some antidepressant medications are secreted in breast milk and would be passed to the baby via this route. Depression at this time can affect the bonding process between a mother and her child because a depressed mother may be less able to interact with her baby or respond in a warm and consistent manner. Unfortunately, her feelings about this can exacerbate and prolong her depression and she may express views that she is a bad mother. It is easy to see how such self-criticism makes it difficult for the new mother and those around her to cope with the depression.

Given that interventions for the mother will also help the well-being of the child there are many clinical programmes aimed at the early recognition and treatment of post-natal depression. Many obstetric and midwifery services use screening questionnaires to try to detect the problem as early as possible. This type of work has identified some very important issues with regard to the timing of onset of depressive symptoms. Contrary to the assumption that all women who wanted to become pregnant will be very content and happy throughout, it seems that many of the symptoms of so-called post-natal depressions can actually begin during the antenatal period. This finding has significant implications for the support and care offered to pregnant women and suggests that screening programmes need to commence earlier.

As discussed in Chapter 4, if a pregnant woman begins to experience depressive symptoms in the antenatal period it is likely that her stress hormone system is more active. Furthermore, the direct connections between the mother and baby (via the placenta) means that this hormonal overactivity can in some cases have an effect on the child's responses to stress in their early life (because the hormones can cross the placenta and influence the development of the stress hormone system of the infant). Taken together this research emphasizes that treating depression associated with pregnancy and childbirth is important for both short-term and long-term well-being of the woman and the child.

Puerperal or post-partum psychosis is an uncommon condition, occurring in about one in 1,000 pregnancies. It is thought to be related to bipolar disorder and the symptoms may be accompanied by loss of reality or psychotic symptoms (hallucinations and delusions), and frequently by ideas of suicide or fear of harming the baby. The problem has been well recognized throughout history and the first psychiatric descriptions are attributed to Osiander in 1797. A description of the condition by Gooch that was written in the 1830s gives a flavour of the disorder: 'the patient swears, bellows, recites poetry, talks bawdy and kicks up such a row that there is the devil to pay in the house'.

In a paper on the history of psychiatry, Hilary Marland provides an elegant review of the case notes of women diagnosed as suffering from puerperal insanity in asylums in the 19th century. Marland reports that many different stages of puerperal mania were described including states which are no longer recognized, such as dullness and relapse into drollery. Importantly, it is clear that the illness was often viewed in a judgemental way, being regarded as associated with sexuality and contravention of codes of decent female behaviour and maternal duty. Puerperal Insanity was attributed to the physical nature of childbirth but also to social factors such as poverty, poor nutrition, difficult family relationships, and stress. Treatment included feeding to the point of stoutness as well as rest and nutrition. In English literature, one of the most famous short stories thought to describe puerperal psychosis is *The Yellow Wallpaper* by Charlotte Perkins Gilman. The text has frequently been debated both for its depiction of the illness experience, but also for the conscious or subconscious maltreatment of the woman by her husband and his medical colleagues.

Today, puerperal psychosis is recognized as an extremely serious illness often regarded as a medical emergency requiring inpatient treatment at specialist mother and baby units. Reasons for the

Box 4 Infanticide

In the 19th century a plea of puerperal insanity was used as a defence in cases of infanticide and it was seen as a major public health problem in Europe at the time. To this day, peri-natal depression or puerperal psychoses remain the most common diagnoses associated with infanticide and if recognized by the court are usually associated with a more lenient penalty than other forms of murder.

high level of concern about this problem become apparent through reading several of the published confidential inquiries into maternal deaths (defined as deaths that occur during pregnancy or in the year after the birth of the baby). Documents such as *Why Mothers Die* highlight that tragically suicide is the leading cause of death in new mothers. It is also the commonest cause of mothers killing their children usually in the heart-breaking belief that they are saving their child from future suffering (see Box 4).

Depression in men

Depression has so often been presented as a 'woman's disease' that it is only relatively recently that health promotion and public information campaigns have recognized the need to target messages at the male population in order to improve the identification of depression and to increase the uptake of treatment in men. There are few differences in the nature of the symptoms experienced by men and women who are depressed, but there may be gender differences in how their distress is expressed or how they react to the symptoms. For example, men may be more likely to become withdrawn rather than to seek support from or confide in other people, they may become more outwardly hostile and have a greater tendency to use alcohol to try to cope with their symptoms. It is also clear that it may be more difficult for men to accept that they have a mental health problem and they are more likely to deny it, delay seeking help, or even to refuse help.

There are no reasons for the onset of depression that are unique to men, but some life events do seem to be particularly associated with the development of the problem. For example, becoming unemployed, retirement, and loss of a partner and change of social roles can all be risk factors for depression in men. In addition, chronic physical health problems or increasing disability may also act as a precipitant.

The relationship between physical illness and depression is complex. When people are depressed they may subjectively report that their general health is worse than that of other people; likewise, people who are ill or in pain may react by becoming depressed. Certain medical problems such as an under-functioning thyroid gland (hypothyroidism) may produce symptoms that are virtually indistinguishable from depression. Overall, the rate of depression in individuals with a chronic physical disease is almost three times higher than those without such problems. Evidence shows that depression is associated with an increased risk of developing certain conditions more than others, for example coronary heart disease, stroke, some cancers, and certain types of diabetes. These findings have become increasingly important as research indicates that some of these problems have shared genetic risk factors. Clinically, physicians and psychiatrists now recognize that the outcome of these physical disorders may be improved by treating the depression as well as the medical condition, and many programmes for chronic physical disorders now take this issue into account.

Suicide

A detailed account of the complexity of the underlying causes of suicide, clinical assessment of the risk of suicide, and its management is unrealistic in this short publication. However, it is impossible to write about mood disorders without acknowledging that individuals who are depressed are more likely than any other group in society to kill themselves. In this brief discussion we highlight some of the difficulties in assessing rates of suicide, what is known about current rates of suicide, offer a few comments on controversies (such as suicide rates and economic recession, copycat suicides, etc.), and what strategies actually reduce overall rates of suicide in a population.

A long-standing problem in gathering data about suicide is that many religions and cultures regard it as a sin or an illegal act. This has had several consequences. For example, coroners and other public officials often strive to avoid identifying suspicious deaths as a suicide, meaning that the actual rates of suicide may be under-reported. Also, in countries where suicide is illegal, criminalizing the act means that those left behind often experience further distress and stigmatization. Attitudes have begun to change, but the taboo about this subject has created problems about the collection of data and understanding of the reasons for suicide. Furthermore, perceptions of what constitutes suicide are also being reviewed and debates about assisted dying for those with terminal illnesses and the 'right to die' serve to demonstrate that this is an emotive issue that is always likely to provoke both sympathy and controversy.

According to the World Health Organization one person commits suicide every minute throughout the world; which equates to about one million people annually. All mental disorders carry an increased risk of premature death, but the risks are highest in depression and bipolar disorder where suicide is increased fifteen- to twentyfold compared to the general population. Rates of suicide have increased significantly in the last half-century, but it is also clear that they vary greatly between countries. The lowest annual rates are reported in Muslim and Latin American countries (about 6 suicides per 100,000 persons) and the highest in countries that were previously identified as Eastern Europe (about 30 per 100,000). Men die more often from suicide than women and men also tend to use more violent methods of suicide such as hanging or shooting, whereas women are more likely to take an overdose of medication.

Risk of suicide varies across the lifespan and the two age groups at highest risk are 15–24-year-olds and over 65-year-olds. In Western countries there has been a substantial increase in suicide rates in young men and it is thought that this may be secondary to access to lethal methods such as car exhaust fumes, high alcohol consumption, and lack of access to support or timely help and unemployment. There is some research that shows fluctuations in suicide rates according to variations in economic prosperity and recession, and a recent publication suggested that there were 10,000 additional suicides (over what would be predicted) associated with the recent economic recession in Europe. These findings have some parallels with early theories of suicide that highlight the influence that social factors may have on individuals.

In 1897, Émile Durkheim, a French sociologist, published his study of suicide that argued that the causes of suicide were linked more with social factors than individual characteristics. He observed that the rate of suicide varied with time and place, for example being less common during times of peace than during times of war and more likely in times of economic depression rather than prosperity. He looked for factors that explained variations other than emotional stress, such as the degree to which individuals feel integrated into society and developed a typology to describe different forms of suicide (see Box 5).

Most individuals with depression can and do recover from their illness episode and, even if they experience further relapses, suicide is a rare outcome. Nevertheless, suicide is viewed as a tragic consequence that should be prevented if at all possible and so clinical programmes have been introduced to improve the detection of depression and provide early access to effective

Box 5 Durkheim's typology of suicide

- Anomic suicide: where an individual lacks social direction and is no longer guided by society because it has such a weak effect upon the individual.

- Altuistic suicide: where an individual is strongly integrated into a society which exerts a strong influence on an individual's decision to kill themselves.

- Egoistic suicide: where an individual is not integrated into a society and represents an individual's decision who is no longer dependent on others' control or opinion.

- Fatalistic suicide: which is the result of strict rules in a society which have proved decisive for the destiny of an individual (the opposite of anomic suicide).

treatments especially for vulnerable groups, such as people recently discharged from a psychiatric hospital. These strategies are combined with training to ensure that clinicians ask depressed patients if they have thought about harming themselves. Suggestions that asking such questions would increase the likelihood that the patient would act on ideas of suicide are entirely unfounded, and indeed for most patients being able to talk to a professional about these thoughts is a relief. Whilst ensuring that clinicians identify individuals at increased risk of suicide is vitally important, research suggests that ultimately, the most effective way of decreasing the rates of suicide is to use population-based interventions ranging from guidelines on media reporting through to reducing access to means.

It is difficult to be certain whether the media portrayal of suicide might lead to someone else killing themselves. Evidence for copycat suicides is equivocal, although it is suggested that the risk is especially increased when a famous person is involved.

However, concerns about the risk of copycat suicides are not new, and there are documented examples from previous centuries. For example, there was a spate of copycat suicides in 1774 after the publication of Goethe's novel *Die Leiden des Jungen Werthers* (The Sorrows of Young Werther), which described how a young man killed himself because he was unlucky in love. The book was eventually banned.

More recently, concerns have been voiced that some suicides may have occurred after individuals became distressed as a result of cyber-bullying which includes negative or abusive comments being posted on internet web-pages or circulated via different internet sites. This has led to some attempts to promote guidelines on responsible reporting of suicides in the media and attempts to regulate access to websites or modify the content of unregulated sites (although the latter is difficult to implement).

The most effective strategy for reducing suicide rates is to reduce access to methods for killing oneself. For example, suicide rates are lower in countries with stricter limitations on access to firearms. Also, in the early 20th century placing one's head in a gas oven was a common method of suicide in the United Kingdom, but following the conversion from coal gas to North Sea gas the suicide rate dropped. Following on from this, new car exhausts are now fitted with catalytic converters to reduce deaths by carbon monoxide poisoning.

Restricting access to barbiturates in the 1960s led to a 23 per cent reduction in suicide by these drugs; limiting the purchase of over-the-counter painkillers (analgesics) such as paracetamol and using blister packs to slow ingestion have been found to be effective in some studies. Other public health interventions include the erection of barriers or nets placed in suicide hotspots such as the Clifton Suspension Bridge in Bristol in the United Kingdom and the Golden Gate Bridge in San Francisco in the USA (see Figure 3). Telephone helplines such as the Samaritans provide the

CRISIS COUNSELING

**THERE IS HOPE
MAKE THE CALL**

**THE CONSEQUENCES OF
JUMPING FROM THIS
BRIDGE ARE FATAL
AND TRAGIC.**

3. The crisis counselling sign on Golden Gate Bridge in San Francisco.

opportunity for people to talk in confidence in the hope this will
prevent them from acting on suicidal thoughts and signs
displaying telephone helpline numbers are displayed on many
high-level bridges.

Chapter 4
Models of depression

Epidemiological studies of depression give important insights into populations at higher risk of depression. For example, the prevalence of depression is higher in groups living in socially adverse conditions, and is higher in those with a recent experience of bereavement. However, not everyone in these circumstances will develop a clinical depression. Theories about the causes of depressive illnesses can help to clarify the reasons for these individual differences. Here, we highlight some of the best-known biological, psychological, and social models and then discuss attempts to integrate these into a multi-dimensional theory.

Biological models: monoamine and neuro-endocrine hypotheses

The initial chemical imbalance model of depression arose by serendipity. In the mid-20th century, reports began to appear that suggested that a number of medications used to treat medical problems could increase or decrease symptoms of depression. Knowledge of how these drugs affected the amount of different chemical molecules in the brain led to the development of the monoamine hypothesis of depression. To understand this, it is useful to briefly outline how messages are transmitted through the nervous system.

Many brain regions are important in the regulation of emotions. Communication between these regions and with the rest of the body occurs via the nervous system. Each neuron (nerve cell) comprises a cell body with an axon (like a tail) that has many dendrites (branches). Multiple communication pathways are established through the development of connections between networks of dendrites, and some nerve cells increase the activity of neurons in their network, whilst others decrease responses (called inhibitory neurons). Nerve cells are not in direct contact with each other, they are separated by a small gap called a synapse, and information is passed across the synapse by a molecule called a neurotransmitter (chemical messenger). When the electric impulse passes down the axon it leads to the release of the neurotransmitter from a vesicle (storage area). This molecule 'docks' with a receptor on the next cell and the message is transferred across the network (see Figure 4). The receptors are deactivated between messages and the neurotransmitter is released from the dock back into the synapse from where it is reabsorbed into the neuron from which it originated (a process referred to as re-uptake). There are at least thirty neurotransmitters, but the subgroup called monoamines that include norepinephrine, dopamine, and serotonin are regarded as particularly important in depression. It is suggested that serotonin regulates many important functions in the body such as sleep, eating, and mood; norepinephrine is implicated in stress reactions and alertness and energy and interest in life, and dopamine levels may influence motivation, pleasure, and 'reward-seeking' behaviour. Also, it is suggested that changes in serotonin may promote or reduce norepinephrine activity.

In the 1950s, separate observations were reported regarding the effects on mood, energy, and appetite of a new anti-hypertensive drug and a new anti-tuberculosis medication. Reserpine was introduced as a treatment for high blood pressure, but about 15 per cent of individuals receiving it reported experiencing significant levels of depression, sometimes accompanied by

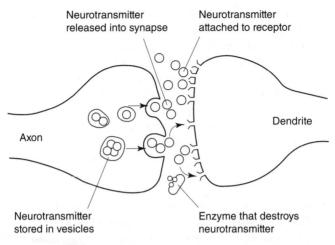

Neurotransmitter released into synapse

Neurotransmitter attached to receptor

Dendrite

Axon

Neurotransmitter stored in vesicles

Enzyme that destroys neurotransmitter

4. A synapse in the nervous system.

thoughts of suicide. In contrast, individuals in a sanatorium on Staten Island in the USA who received iproniazid as a treatment for tuberculosis reported feeling happier, more energized, and their appetite improved. Although these drugs were apparently unconnected, it was established that they acted on the same neurotransmitter systems in the brain and that reserpine reduced the circulating levels of monoamines, whilst iproniazid increased the levels (by preventing the action of monoamine oxidase, an enzyme that reduces the amount of monoamine neurotransmitters available in neurons).

The monoamine theory of depression was very popular in the 1960s and 1970s, and it was suggested that a deficiency in monoamines available in the synapse (either because of underactive production or overactive breakdown of these neurotransmitters) could explain the observed symptoms of depression. There were slight differences in views regarding whether the most important disturbance was in norepinephrine (favoured in the USA) or in serotonin (favoured in Europe), but support for the notion of monoamine 'imbalances' was provided by research on animals and humans. The latter included post-mortem studies demonstrating differences in monoamine levels in depressed versus non-depressed individuals and the experimental effects on mood and activity of drugs that alter monoamine levels. In addition, studies of individuals who had died by suicide showed reductions in monoamines in some regions of the brain thought to be associated with emotional regulation. The findings from these studies and enthusiasm for this apparent biological cause of depression led to the introduction of antidepressant medications that increased the availability of monoamines in synapses.

Published critiques of the monoamine hypothesis frequently highlight the dangers of the selective focus on so few of the neurotransmitters that operate in the brain, as there is limited information on what the other 90 per cent of chemical messengers are doing during this process. Also, in animal studies it is clear that monoamines influence multiple behaviours not just those that might be interpreted as being depression related. Most international researchers are aware of these weaknesses in a model of depression that implicated a single neurotransmitter system and even Schildkraut, who was one of the first American scientists to describe the monoamine theory, was quoted as saying the theory was 'undoubtedly, at best, a reductionist oversimplification of a very complex biological state'.

The monoamine theory was instrumental in the development of depression-specific medications, but the widespread use of antidepressants has exposed other flaws in the model. The most obvious is that not all medications that alter monoamine levels produced the anticipated mood or behavioural effects. Also, there is a time-lag of about two weeks between increases in monoamine levels and evidence of changes in depressive symptoms that cannot be fully explained by the model and may indicate that the monoamine changes are a secondary or downstream effect of some other primary biological process. Partly in response to this, later revisions of the model shifted away from a focus on the amount of neurotransmitter available in the synapse to the importance of receptor sensitivity, suggesting deficiencies in docking system may be more germane. Also, scientists have highlighted that the neurotransmitter systems have important links with other neural pathways and the neuro-endocrine (hormone) system.

Another key biological model of depression is the neuro-endocrine hypothesis. A range of hormones have been implicated in the causes of depression and individuals with endocrine disorders such as hypothyroidism are at increased risk of depression. Whilst disturbances in several hormones (e.g. thyroid hormones, testosterone, oestrogen, progesterone) have been associated with depression, most research has focused on the regulation of stress responses through the linkages within the hypothalamic-pituitary-adrenal axis (HPA axis), an important system connecting the nervous system and the endocrine system.

The endocrine system consists of a number of organs in the body such as the thyroid and adrenal glands that help regulate many body functions through the release of hormones into the bloodstream. The hormones are produced in response to messages from the brain and the levels of different hormones fluctuate in a predictable way at certain stages of life (e.g. sex hormone levels change at puberty) and also during the course of the day (e.g. varying over the 24-hour sleep–wake cycle). Unlike neurotransmitters, the messengers that control the first link in the chain between the brain and the endocrine glands are molecules (peptides) called releasing factors. Releasing factors are produced in a brain region called the hypothalamus (a key structure for regulating hormone secretion) and send messages to the pituitary gland which in turn prompts the release of hormones from endocrine glands. The increased levels of circulating hormones in the bloodstream regulate a number of processes around the body, but also influence the activity of the neuro-endocrine system and prevent the overproduction of hormones via a feedback loop.

Serotonin, norepinephrine, and dopamine receptors are all present in the hypothalamus, suggesting connections between the activity of the monoamine system and the regulation of hormones. Furthermore, these monoamine pathways link the amygdala and hippocampus (brain structures known to play a critical role in emotional regulation) to the neuro-endocrine system. In day-to-day life, hormone levels change when the body responds to acute stress. For example, higher levels of adrenalin are produced when a person encounters any sort of anxiety provoking event, which can range from public speaking to life threatening situations, etc. In these circumstances a person's heart rate may increase, they may begin to feel dizzy or nauseous, and they may become hyper-vigilant (the so-called flight or fight response).

Interestingly, the brain responds to chronic adversity or sustained stress by producing a different sequence of hormones. First, corticotrophin releasing factor (CRF) is released from the hypothalamus. This in turn increases the production of adreno-corticotrophic hormone (ACTH) from the pituitary and ACTH regulates the release of cortisol (a stress hormone) from the adrenal gland. Cortisol has wide-ranging effects around the body including significant effects on metabolism (e.g. delivering fuel to muscles) as well as affecting behaviour via its links with numerous brain regions (see Figure 5).

The difference between normal and abnormal adaptation to chronic stress is that in the latter scenario the normal feedback loop does not function as expected. This has several implications, for example CRF levels appear to be important in 'fear conditioning' and the development of emotional memories of reward and punishment. Most importantly, the HPA system is no longer turned off by high levels of circulating cortisol and the normal daily variation in the amount of cortisol in the bloodstream is lost. Persistently high levels of cortisol are not good for many brain cells, and may speed up the usual rate of death of some neurons and have negative effects on memory and learning. In addition, these high levels of cortisol can

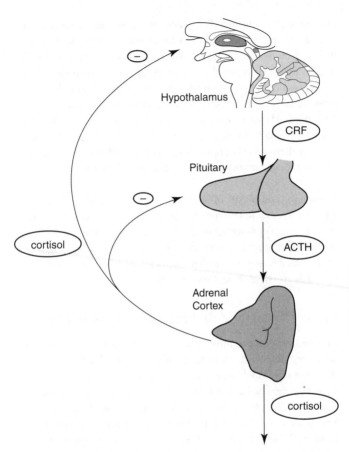

5. The Hypothalamic-Pituitary-Adrenal Axis and the 'normal' negative feedback loop.

be associated with reduced levels of the neurotransmitters linked to mood regulation.

The changes in mood, appetite, and energy seen in these abnormal responses to stress resemble the core features of clinical depression, leading many researchers to propose that disturbed HPA axis functioning was the underlying cause of depression. At one point in the 1980s, it was hoped that a laboratory investigation that measures the functioning of the HPA axis and the feedback system (called the dexamethasone suppression test) might provide a diagnostic test for depression. However, whilst animal and human models of depression demonstrate abnormalities in the HPA axis, not all individuals who experience depression show such abnormalities and some individuals who do demonstrate HPA axis abnormalities do not have depression but have other mental health problems such as anxiety, bipolar, or post-traumatic stress disorders, etc.

Despite the complexity of unravelling the cause and effects of altered HPA axis functioning in depression it remains an important focus for international research. Many ongoing studies are exploring whether targeting the functioning of this axis might enable the development of new medications that can reduce the risk of depression or treat its symptoms.

Psychological models: Beck's cognitive model

Although several cognitive and behavioural theories of depression have been described, we focus mainly on Aaron Beck's model. Beck, who qualified in medicine at Brown University in the USA, is usually regarded as the founding father of Cognitive Behaviour Therapy (CBT). Beck developed an interest in psychotherapy at a time when there was a shift towards behavioural models of emotional disorders, partly driven by the failure to demonstrate a scientific basis for psychoanalysis. Beck attempted to find evidence in support of psychoanalytic theories, but his research on thinking and cognition in patients with depression undermined the notion of unconscious motivations. Beck found that the content of an individual's conscious thoughts and the ways in which they processed information offered a far more powerful explanation of the experiences described by depressed patients and during the 1960s Beck wrote his seminal papers on depression detailing a cognitive model of emotional disorders (see Figure 6).

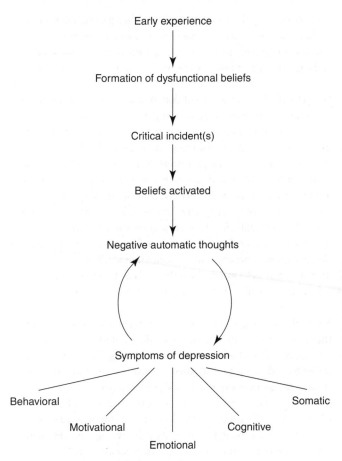

6. Beck's Cognitive Model of Depression.

Beck's model offers a continuity hypothesis, which is to say that the
model suggests that disorders such as depression are exaggerated
forms of normal emotional responses such as sadness. It also
views emotional and behavioural responses to events or experiences
as being largely determined by the cognitive appraisal made by
the individual, for example, social avoidance may arise if a person

experiences negative thoughts such as 'other people will find me boring'. The model includes two critical elements related to information-processing—cognitive structures (thoughts and beliefs) and cognitive mechanisms (called systematic errors in reasoning).

In Beck's model, it is proposed that an individual's interpretations of events or experiences are encapsulated in automatic thoughts, which arise immediately following the event or even at the same time. The difference from a Freudian model is that Beck suggested that these automatic thoughts occur at a conscious level and can be accessible to the individual, although they may not be actively aware of them because they are not concentrating on them. The appraisals that occur in specific situations largely determine the person's emotional and behavioural responses, and this sequence is referred to as the Event-Thought-Feeling-Behaviour link. Furthermore, in depression, the content of a person's thinking is dominated by negative views of themselves, their world, and their future (the so-called negative cognitive triad).

Beck's theory suggests that the themes included in the automatic thoughts are generated via the activation of underlying cognitive structures, called dysfunctional beliefs (or cognitive schemata). All individuals develop a set of rules or 'silent assumptions' derived from early learning experiences. Whilst automatic thoughts are momentary, event-specific cognitions, the underlying beliefs operate across a variety of situations and are more permanent. Most of the underlying beliefs held by the average individual are quite adaptive and guide our attempts to act and react in a considered way. Individuals at risk of depression are hypothesized to hold beliefs that are maladaptive and can have an unhelpful influence on them. Such beliefs may be dormant for long periods but become reactivated by a so-called critical incident, namely an event that carries a specific meaning for that person (and has parallels to the events or experiences that led to the initial development of the belief). For example, an individual who experienced emotional neglect as a child may develop a negative belief that they are unlovable and this belief may be reactivated by an experience of personal rejection.

In depression, the automatic thoughts represent biased appraisals of external events or internal stimuli (arising from within the body), and the conviction that these thoughts are accurate reflections of reality is maintained by systematic errors in reasoning. This means that an individual may selectively focus on or screen out information from their environment that either supports or refutes their view of themselves and their world. For example, in someone who is depressed, the failure of a friend to return a telephone call may lead to 'jumping to conclusions' and focusing on the thought that the person no longer values the friendship (rather than considering other plausible explanations such as their friend was very busy or is notoriously forgetful). Importantly, this faulty information processing contributes to further deterioration in a person's mood, which sets up a vicious cycle with more negative mood increasing the risk of negative interpretations of day-to-day life experiences and these negative cognitions worsening the depressed mood.

Beck suggested that the underlying beliefs that render an individual vulnerable to depression may be broadly categorized into beliefs about being helpless or unlovable. Thus events that are deemed uncontrollable or involve relationship difficulties may be important in the genesis of depressive symptoms. Beliefs about 'the self' seem especially important in the maintenance of depression, particularly when connected with low or variable self-esteem.

A common criticism of Beck's model is that the automatic thoughts and reasoning errors might not precede the development of the depressive episode but may actually be a consequence of a negative mood shift. This has long been acknowledged by Beck, who stated that whilst the vicious cycle of negative thinking leading to low mood and then to further negative thinking may represent a causal theory in some cases, it can be a perpetuating factor in other forms of depression. A further unresolved issue is whether maladaptive underlying belief patterns are separate vulnerability factors for depression, or represent the individual's temperament or personality style. Furthermore, dysfunctional beliefs are reported in a range of mental health problems and, as with the biological models, key elements of the model may not specifically predict depression.

Over the last forty years, there have been a number of developments and revisions of the cognitive model, with increasing attention to cognitive-emotional regulation. For example, one 'response coping style' that can amplify negative mood states is called rumination. A ruminative response style that includes reflection and distancing oneself from a situation to gain sufficient perspective and reduce the negative effect on oneself is not necessarily problematic. However, in some individuals rumination takes the form of toxic brooding on issues, with the individual constantly asking the question 'why does this happen to me?', becoming preoccupied with their own negative feelings and being unable to escape the negative cognitive-emotional loop. This response, sometimes described by the phrase 'getting depressed about being depressed', also tends to reduce the likelihood that a person can actively engage in solving their problems and this response style is closely linked to the onset and maintenance of depression. As such, rumination offers an important potential target for the new models of CBT that are being developed and is also relevant to models used in mindfulness.

Social models: Brown and Harris's studies of depression in women

A moment of reflection about some of the social factors that may increase the risk of developing a depressive disorder leads to the conclusion that many of them are interrelated and likely to occur at the same time. This is particularly true with regard to issues such as unemployment, low socio-economic status, and poor housing, which can be interlinked in a variety of ways. As such, researchers initially found it difficult to disentangle these macro-level phenomena and it was hard to gain a clear understanding of the unique aspects of any individual's experience of their social circumstances; the quality of their core social roles; and the differences in the personal meanings of the life events they reported. A British psychologist called George Brown and a sociologist called Tyrell Harris undertook a series of studies during the 1970s and 1980s that began to link social and psychological perspectives and to understand how these could increase a person's susceptibility to depression. A key element of the studies was the implementation of new types of research interviews that examined the unique individual meaning of any life events and the social difficulties described.

In the initial study, the research team interviewed women in South London, and found that nearly 10 per cent had developed a depressive disorder during the previous year and that nine out of ten of those who became depressed reported serious adversity (negative life events such as domestic violence or ongoing difficulties such as caring for a parent with dementia). In contrast, serious adversity was reported by only a small proportion of the women who had not become depressed. The researchers also found that although there was a much higher rate of depression among working-class women, this only occurred among those with children at home. The women in Brown and Harris's study, who lacked social support from an intimate relationship in their life, were four times more likely to become depressed in the face of these negative experiences (see Box 6). The researchers proposed that the women who experienced depression in the face of these life events were more likely to report a set of specific vulnerability factors; findings which were published in a seminal book called *Social origins of depression: a study of psychiatric disorder in women.*

Box 6 George Brown's vulnerability factors in women

- having three or more children under the age of 14 years
- having no paid employment outside of the home
- a lack of a confiding relationship.
- loss of her mother before the age of 11 years

The second study concentrated on working-class women with a child living at home. Over 400 mothers living in Islington, an inner-city area in north London, were interviewed and anyone who was currently depressed was excluded from the study. One year later over 300 women were interviewed again and the researchers explored social and psychological experiences associated with new onsets of depression. The findings concerning life events were particularly thought-provoking as the researchers uncovered some important caveats that may explain different reactions to similar events and the nature of events linked to onset of depression and also to recovery. For example, the study confirmed that severe threatening events, especially those concerning loss, were important precipitants of depression in women with one or more of the identified vulnerability factors (listed in Box 6).

Interestingly, the use of more refined assessment procedures allowed the researchers to uncover that life events that could be categorized as 'humiliation' or 'entrapment' experiences were particularly associated with the onset of a depressive episode. Loss events which did not involve humiliation were more than 50 per cent less likely to be followed by the onset of depression. The match between such events and the shame felt by some women seemed to be explained by underlying low self-esteem. Also, the researchers reported that even in depressed women who were experiencing difficulties in one area of their life (such as marital difficulties), a 'fresh start event' in another life domain (such as starting a college course) often seemed to help to set them on the pathway to recovery. Taken together, these findings offered important insights into differences in the predisposition to develop depression, the risk factors that may precipitate a specific depressive episode, but also social events that might modify the course of illness and be associated with recovery.

Biopsychosocial models

Whilst media pronouncements on theories about depression take polarized views of the literature, researchers are more inclined to acknowledge that there are important overlaps between elements of psychological, social, and biological models. For example, the concept of matching events in women at risk of depression described in Brown and Harris's work is very similar to Beck's notion that it is the life events with a specific personal meaning for an individual that activate underlying beliefs and set off the cycle of depression.

The neuro-endocrine and monoamine models highlight that these two biological systems are connected and therefore affect the regulation of neurotransmitter and stress hormones. They also emphasize the importance of the level of stress in an individual's social and family environment, recognizing that life events or chronic adversity are potent causes of changes in the nervous and neuro-endocrine systems.

The four theories described highlight the interaction between stress and vulnerability factors, but in order to integrate these approaches more fully it is useful to consider the origins of the vulnerabilities. For example, why are some individuals more likely to manifest monoamine dysfunctions or to have an HPA axis that is more sensitive to stressors, and why do some people develop dysfunctional and unhelpful underlying beliefs?

Figure 7 offers a simple representation of the stress-vulnerability model. This simple schematic identifies that under extreme stress

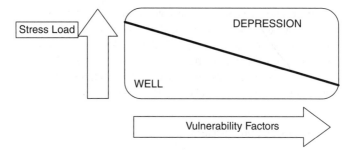

7. A simple representation of a stress–vulnerability model.

anyone might experience a depressive episode, but it does not differentiate the different elements of vulnerability. To provide a snapshot of some of the ongoing difficulties of differentiating 'nature versus nurture', we will briefly highlight current ideas on gene-environment interactions and how the many different systems in the body may interact. We begin by examining research on families, then genes and the environment.

Family research

Depression runs in families, and research from around the world robustly and repeatedly shows that the children of a parent who has a history of depression have a two- to fourfold increase in their risk for developing a depressive episode, and a family history in more than one generation (e.g. in parents and grandparents) not only increases the risk of depression, it increases the likelihood that the depression may start earlier in life. However, these findings do not prove that depression is inherited. For example, living with a depressed parent may adversely affect family interactions and might increase the likelihood that other family members would also become depressed. Having several generations affected within a family may mean each generation has developed certain patterns of behaviour or so-called coping styles that affect the family environment in such a way as to increase the likelihood that the next generation may also be at risk of depression.

Depression

Genetic vulnerability

To clarify genetic vulnerability to depression it is helpful to examine the genetic makeup of a group of relatives and one of the best methods for doing this is to consider twin studies. Twins can be identical (monozygotic) sharing 100 per cent of their genes in common or non-identical (dizygotic) sharing 50 per cent of their genes in common, and therefore being no more genetically alike than brothers and sisters. Using this knowledge, researchers ascertain the rates of depression in one member of the twin pair, and then investigate how frequently the second twin also reports a depressive episode. The frequency of depression in both twins in one pair is termed the concordance rate. If genetic factors are relevant then the concordance rates in the identical twins should be higher than those in non-identical twins, and the rates of depression in the latter group should be about the same as seen in other family members who share 50 per cent of their genes in common, such as siblings and parents.

One such study of over 100 twin pairs that was undertaken at the Maudsley Hospital in London showed that identical twins had concordance rates of about 46 per cent for depression compared with about 20 per cent in non-identical twins. Similar findings have been shown in other twin studies and they highlight two very significant issues with regard to genetic vulnerability or inheritance. First, they show that genetic factors are important in the risk of developing depression and second, that even if an individual shares 100 per cent of their genes in common with someone who has developed depression, that does not mean they will experience a depressive episode. The latter is worth emphasizing as it means that genetic factors alone cannot explain the occurrence of depression, but that social, psychological, and environmental factors are also important in determining which individuals with genetic vulnerability to depression actually experience a clinical episode.

To help people understand this information, it is useful to briefly consider what 'genetic risk' actually means. The genes inherited via our parents are important in determining many of our physical characteristics or traits such as hair colour, and genes can also influence our personality characteristics. However, at a basic level, genes control biological processes, and in reality many genes, often interacting in complex ways, influence the expression of a particular trait. There is not a single gene linked to a specific behaviour or a particular emotional state. As such we will never find a gene that dictates that one person is an introvert or another is an extrovert. By the same token, there will never be a 'gene for depression' or a 'gene for schizophrenia'. A more plausible model is that: (a) some mental processes and behaviours are more strongly inherited than others, but that (b) even when genetic factors are involved, there are likely to be many genes that play a part and that (c) each individual gene only has a small influence on the final picture. Also, just to make matters even more complicated, the activities of many genes can be turned on or turned off in different environments.

Despite the complexities of genetic coding, some interesting findings have emerged, including evidence from the Human Genome project that genes on certain chromosomes (e.g. on genes 12, 15q, etc.) may be more strongly linked to depression than expected by chance alone. Furthermore, some researchers have reported associations between genes that influence serotonin receptors and those that influence monoamine oxidase (the enzyme that influences the breakdown of monoamines and can be associated with depression). However, these findings should be viewed with caution as it is often the case that initially promising linkages are not replicated in later studies.

An example of replicating research findings comes from a study by a group of researchers led by a psychiatrist called Caspi. In 2003, they reported that they had identified a connection between a gene that regulates serotonin and an individual's ability to bounce back from a significant traumatic experience such as childhood abuse or neglect (i.e. their resilience). The researchers undertook a long-term community study that assessed individuals prospectively for many years from the age of about 3 years until around 25 years of age and found that individuals who had one variant of a serotonin transporter gene (without getting too technical, it is called 5HTTLPR-S) developed more depression or were more likely to express suicidal ideas in response to stressful life events than individuals who had another variant (called 5HTTLPR-L). Further research showed that individuals who had the 'S' variant also showed increased activity in a brain region called the amygdala (known to be involved in emotional regulation) when exposed to 'threatening stimuli' under laboratory conditions. These findings seemed to offer evidence of a gene-by-environment interaction, in which an individual's response to environmental events is moderated by their genetic makeup, and that the genes were acting on their neurotransmitters (and indirectly on the HPA axis) in areas of the brain that regulate emotional responses.

Psychiatry researchers took notice and the journal *Science* declared that it was one of the most important discoveries in the field of mental health. However, not all subsequent research has replicated these findings and so it is unclear how robust the links are between the serotonin transporter genes and the development of depression following environmental stress. The important take home message is that any research that tries to uncover the links between depression, genes, and the environment will need to explain not just which gene might be important but *how* that gene mediates the relationship between causes and effects. In that respect, the association between a gene that regulates a monoamine that is implicated in emotional regulation and the finding that the stress (HPA axis) response is exaggerated in the carriers of that gene at least provides a template for future research.

Environmental effects

Unique environmental effects that may increase the risk of depression are not limited to the offspring of depressed parents and can operate in a number of ways in a range of social contexts.

For example, the development of an individual's personality will be influenced by their early parent–child interactions such as the development of secure attachments, experiences of separation, and the 'emotional temperature' of their environment (such as levels of parental affection or control) as well as by their genetic makeup. Some examples are given to illustrate the potential impact of early social experiences.

In Chapter 3 we commented that post-natal depression is sometimes a misnomer, as many of these women are shown to have symptoms of depression that commence in the antenatal period. Several studies suggest that stress during pregnancy can have a negative impact on the offspring, for example they may be more at risk of premature birth. Also, there may be a direct effect on the development of the HPA axis of the child; a hypothesis known as the set point theory. In utero, foetal development is influenced by the intrauterine environment and high levels of maternal stress hormones (which can pass across the placenta into the foetal bloodstream) may influence the development of systems in the baby such as the HPA axis. This can mean that the child develops a more sensitive HPA system that produces more cortisol in response to stress and other adverse experiences than other individuals.

A number of adverse events in childhood increase the risk of depression in adulthood. These can be related to several deprivations some of which may be linked to social circumstances such as poor nutrition, but also to social and emotional neglect. There is emerging evidence that these experiences can influence the development of the serotonergic system and also the sensitivity of the HPA axis (as many of these systems continue to develop throughout childhood). For example, it has been shown that adult women with a history of childhood abuse who were currently depressed exhibited increased cortisol levels in response to stress, as compared with abused women without depression, or with healthy controls (i.e. women who did not report abuse or depression). Also, there was a positive correlation between the ACTH and cortisol responses to stress, the magnitude of abuse, and the severity of depression. The researchers interpreted the findings as demonstrating that the depressed women with a history of abuse had a chronically overactive HPA system, suggesting it then took less stress to 'tip them over the edge' than might be the case for other individuals.

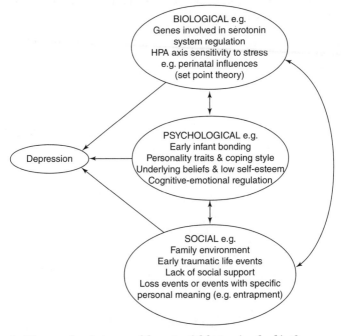

8. **Diagram showing some of the potential factors involved in the development of depression.**

In summary, this chapter aims to demonstrate that unidimensional models, such as the monoamine hypothesis or the social origins of depression model, are important building blocks for understanding depression. However, in reality there is no one cause and no single pathway to depression and, as shown in Figure 8, multiple factors increase vulnerability to depression. Whether or not someone at risk of depression actually develops the disorder is partly dictated by whether they are exposed to certain types of life events, the perceived level of threat or distress associated with those events (which in turn is influenced by cognitive and emotional reactions and temperament), their ability to cope with these experiences (their resilience or adaptability under stress), and the functioning of their biological stress-sensitivity systems (including the thresholds for switching on their body's stress responses).

Chapter 5
The evolution of treatments

In Chapters 1 and 2 we tried to demonstrate that depression has been recognized throughout history. In ancient times, the problem was called melancholia to signify its association with black bile and humoral imbalances. Treatments that existed were largely targeted at restoring balance, for example, through the use of herbs and concoctions, of purgatives to flush out toxins from the gut, or of leeches to remove impurities from the blood. In the Middle Ages, when underlying physical causes of melancholia were rejected, treatments were targeted at the supernatural or evil forces that were assumed to have possessed the person, leading to punitive interventions ranging from the use of the earliest forms of straitjackets to witch-hunts. In the 17th and 18th centuries, mechanical and circulatory theories of the causes of melancholia increased in popularity. Treatments included mechanical devices to induce vomiting (e.g. whirling chairs) or swing chairs to excite the patient and overcome apathy.

The earliest individual treatments that were devised had little or no chance of succeeding as the ideas about the causes of depression bore minimal resemblance to what we now think (such as discussed in Chapter 4). As such, the major intervention for many centuries involved the removal of the individual with melancholia from their home environment. The first known asylums came into existence in Baghdad in about AD 705 and

Muslim physicians were renowned for their humane approaches to patients. In Europe, monasteries were the main source of care until asylums began to be introduced in the 1300s. However, the primary role of these institutions was to provide custodial care to keep people with mental illnesses away from society, and it was not until the 18th century that reformers such as Pinel in France and William Tuke in England began to change the role of asylums into more therapeutic environments.

By the turn of the 20th century, when Kraepelin's classification of mental disorders held sway, individuals with manic depression and melancholia were still more likely to be admitted to an asylum. However, the diagnosis of depression was now applied to a much broader spectrum of individuals, many of whom had conditions that fitted into Freud's view of neuroses and more and more of these individuals were treated in outpatient settings.

To give a flavour of the evolution of interventions for depression in the 21st century, we will first discuss the treatments that were introduced for people admitted to asylums such as sedation (barbiturates, insulin coma therapy) and physical treatments (electroconvulsive therapy, trans-cranial magnetic stimulation, and psychosurgery). This is followed by a discussion of the development of the medications used today for inpatients and outpatients, such as antidepressants and the mood stabilizer lithium. Finally, we discuss psychotherapies, which are primarily used as a treatment for outpatients.

Sedative treatments

The early drugs used in psychiatry were sedatives, as calming a patient was probably the only treatment that was feasible and available. Also, it made it easier to manage large numbers of individuals with small numbers of staff at the asylum. Morphine, hyoscine, chloral, and later bromide were all used in this way. The induction of sleep with bromide was first tried as a psychiatric treatment by Neil Macleod, a psychiatrist in Edinburgh in 1899. He used bromide for a patient suffering from acute mania who slept for days and then awoke 'cured'. However, bromide sleep was soon abandoned as bromide was found to be toxic and there were fatalities. In the 1920s, a Swiss psychiatrist, Klaesi, used barbiturates to induce prolonged sleep and as a way of calming patients to improve the rapport between patient and doctor and increase the possibility that they could engage in psychotherapy. This treatment became popular, but again a number of deaths led to its discontinuation, although the outpatient use and abuse of barbiturates continued for many decades. In the USA Henry Stack Sullivan (a psychoanalyst) also suggested the use of alcohol to calm patients sufficiently to allow them to participate in psychotherapy.

Insulin coma therapy came into vogue in the 1930s following the work of Manfred Sakel, a doctor working in a private sanatorium in Berlin. He noted that insulin injections (a hormone that regulates blood glucose levels) led patients being treated for opiate addiction to become less agitated. Also, if the doses of insulin were increased the patients went into a coma after which they were much calmer and less irritable. Sakel initially proposed this treatment as a cure for schizophrenia, but its use gradually spread to mood disorders to the extent that asylums in Britain opened so-called insulin units. These were specially designed to administer the treatment for one to three hours at a time, often persisting for two to three months (or sixty or more sessions). Recovery from the coma required administration of glucose, but complications were common and death rates ranged from 1–10 per cent.

Insulin coma therapy was initially viewed as having tremendous benefits, but later re-examinations have highlighted that the results could also be explained by a placebo effect associated with the dramatic nature of the process or, tragically, because deprivation of glucose supplies to the brain may have reduced the person's reactivity because it had induced permanent damage.

Physical treatments: from shock therapies to vagal nerve stimulation

A number of 'shock therapies' (later called electroconvulsive treatment or ECT) are described throughout the ages. However, their development from the 1930s onwards was initially stimulated by the now disproved hypothesis that individuals with schizophrenia or other severe mental disorders such as manic depression did not suffer from epilepsy. This notion led to an assumption that inducing convulsions in those with severe mental disorders could then lead to the reduction in symptoms. It was an Italian professor of psychiatry, Ugo Cerletti, and his assistant (Lucio Bini) who were the first people to use electricity rather than chemicals such as camphor to produce an epileptic fit in humans.

Despite the hypothesis for the mechanism of action of ECT being wrong, it was noted to be effective in reducing symptoms of depression and became very widely used in the 1940s and 1950s. Originally, ECT was given without anaesthetic and was associated with complications such as bone fractures because of the dramatic epileptic fits that were produced. Unsurprisingly, it became a feared treatment and was widely regarded as punitive. There are many graphic descriptions in Western literature of its use as a punishment and its lasting, negative effects (e.g. *Clockwork Orange*; *One Flew over the Cuckoo's Nest*) and several famous writers talk of their negative personal experiences of ECT such as Sylvia Plath, in *The Bell Jar*. The unmodified versions of ECT also had side effects such as memory loss, which the writer Ernest Hemingway complained bitterly about.

Although public surveys suggest some softening of attitudes towards the modified type of ECT used today, it remains the source of much controversy. It is primarily used for severe depression or mania if these problems do not respond to other treatments. The procedures have been refined radically from the earliest primitive interventions depicted in the cinema. For example, an anaesthetic is given so that the patient is unconscious, there is no longer any visible evidence of a convulsion, and the process is closely monitored by measuring the electrical activity of the brain. Whilst these modifications have made ECT somewhat more acceptable to patients and their families, the lack of clarity about how ECT works means that concerns remain. The present hypothesis is that the seizure makes the receptors (docking systems for chemical messengers in the brain) of the brain cells more sensitive to the effects of the messenger chemicals, which in turn send stronger signals around the nervous system and help to correct defective functioning in the neurotransmitter and hormone systems (described in Chapter 3).

In modern psychiatric practice, the main reason for using ECT is that it can produce rapid improvements in symptoms. Hence it is often used when individuals are so depressed that they cannot even eat or drink properly and the depression is no longer a psychiatric crisis but a medical emergency. Interestingly, in those with less severe or less life-threatening episodes of chronic depression, a new treatment, called transcranial magnetic stimulation (TMS), is increasingly being used. This does not require anaesthesia; an electromagnetic coil is placed over the scalp and uses magnetic fields to stimulate nerve cells in the brain to improve symptoms of depression.

The development of psychosurgery as a treatment for mental illness arose from evidence that industrial accidents that caused brain damage may be associated with changes in temperament and could render people calmer than they had appeared previously. From the 1890s onwards, observers suggested that similar brain changes could be reproduced surgically by severing the connections between the frontal lobes and the rest of the brain and that this could be used as a treatment for severe anxiety and depression as it would reduce emotional responsivity. In 1935, the Portuguese neurologist Antonio Moniz described a surgical procedure called 'leucotomy' where part of the frontal lobes of the brain was destroyed using an instrument called a 'leucotome'. Moniz claimed great success for leucotomy operations and was awarded a Nobel Prize in 1949.

In the USA, Walter Freeman and James Watts developed the technique further, which they called 'lobotomy'. Lobotomy did make patients calmer but there was a high price to pay for this, as lobotomy also reduced their judgement and social skills and could cause personality changes. Concern about the risk of abuse of this operation was expressed by the public and in literature and films. A classic and distressing portrayal of its misuse appears in Ken Kesey's novel and the film *One Flew over the Cuckoo's Nest* where lobotomy is performed on the rebellious Randle McMurphy to punish and control him after he has attacked the leader of the inpatient unit, Nurse Ratchet. Few individuals who saw the film can fail to be anti-psychosurgery.

The advent of other treatments and greater scrutiny of the reasons for psychosurgery have been associated with a dramatic decrease in its use in most countries in the last sixty years. During the early 1950s, prefrontal leucotomy was performed on about 14,000 individuals in the United Kingdom, with operations on women outnumbering men by about two to one. By the 1970s fewer than 100 operations were performed each year in the United Kingdom, and currently it is considerably less (10–20 operations per year). Its use is carefully regulated and the procedure is only carried out in specialized centres for highly selected cases after extensive assessments. These defined circumstances usually involve highly distressing and severely debilitating chronic depression or obsessive compulsive disorder for which no other treatment produces any benefits. The procedure has also changed radically, with the crude approaches used in the early operations being superseded by an approach called stereotactic surgery, a computerized procedure which places small electrodes within a selected part of the brain associated with emotional control.

The newest surgical procedure introduced in psychiatry is Vagal Nerve Stimulation (VNS), which was originally introduced for individuals with treatment-refractory epilepsy. Although VNS is not technically a psychosurgery procedure, as it does not involve surgery to the brain, it does involve the surgical implantation of a pacemaker-like device in the body. A wire attached to the device allows the delivery of brief electrical impulses (about 30 seconds or so in duration) to the left vagus nerve in the neck. The vagus nerve has numerous connections to many key regions of the brain and it is believed that stimulation of the vagus nerve modifies the activity of some areas of the brain that are involved in regulating mood. The evidence for the use of VNS is equivocal and it is not recommended in all countries as a treatment for depression. Also, a potential drawback is that the response is slow and the benefits of VNS may not become apparent for nine or more months after the device has been implanted. Currently, its use is reserved for carefully selected individuals with treatment-resistant depression.

Medications: antidepressants and lithium

The general public have long been suspicious about the use of physical treatments for depression that we have described and have repeatedly expressed fears that the treatments will be misused. However, the main reason for the demise of physical treatments was the discovery of drugs to treat specific psychiatric illnesses.

By the 1950s, pharmacology for general medical conditions was developing rapidly. Psychiatrists were also very keen to find drug treatments for use in their speciality, but most discoveries arose as offshoots from research in general medicine. For example, in 1951 Henri Laborit, a surgeon in the French Navy, wanted to find a way of reducing surgical shock in patients which he thought was mainly a consequence of the anaesthetics they were using. Laborit began to experiment with antihistamines and came across chlorpromazine and noticed that patients became less anxious or indifferent to emotions or pain if they had been given this drug. This finding was brought to the attention of Pierre Deniker, who was a psychiatrist, and Deniker and his colleague Jean Delay started to use chlorpromazine in the Hospital of Saint Anne in Paris.

Deniker and Delay reported that chlorpromazine was very helpful for patients with schizophrenia, mania, and very severe depression. Indeed, individuals who had been institutionalized for years were discharged to live normal lives in the community, leading to overoptimistic predictions that this represented a revolutionary treatment that would lead to the closure of psychiatric hospitals. Although chlorpromazine is more relevant to the treatment of schizophrenia than depression, its discovery and introduction for patients with mental disorders changed the face of psychiatric practice and kindled a new-found enthusiasm to find other medications. One of the first antidepressants, called imipramine, had a chemical structure similar to antihistamines.

With the rise of the monoamine theory of depression came the introduction first of tricyclics (so called because the chemical compounds comprised three interconnected chemical rings) and then of the monoamine oxidase inhibitors (so-called because they prevented the activity of the enzyme monoamine oxidase). These classes of medications increased the amount of monoamine available in the synapse, although different medications sometimes worked more on one monoamine than another. The monoamine oxidase inhibitors were more complicated to prescribe as they could interact with foods in the normal diet (such as cheese) and so were less widely used than the tricyclics, but both types of drug remained the mainstay of treatment for many years.

The next antidepressants to be introduced again increased the amount of monoamines available in the brain but produced effects in a slightly different way from the first generation drugs. The new drugs were called selective serotonin reuptake inhibitors (the

SSRIs), of which the most (in)famous is Prozac. Initially viewed as a significant advance with easier prescribing regimes and different side effect profiles from the old drugs (that made the new medications more acceptable to some patients), the SSRIs and all the so-called second generation antidepressants introduced since then have increasingly been scrutinized and criticized by patients and professionals. These negative reactions are fuelled partly by claims that the benefits may have been overstated because of biased reporting of research results, partly because of the marketing strategies that try to extend the use of the drugs to broad populations of patients, and also because of concerns that SSRIs may increase rather than decrease self-harm in some people or be addictive for others. Some of the concerns about SSRIs have not stood the test of time, but, as noted in Chapter 4, suspicions remain about the relative benefits and risks of these medications and the public and media demonstrate huge ambivalence towards these medications (see Figure 9).

It was an Australian psychiatrist John Cade who discovered that lithium carbonate could be used as a mood stabilizer for severe depression and for mania. In the 1940s, Cade developed a theory that there was a toxin responsible for causing mental illness and that the illness abated when the toxin was excreted in urine. Working at the Bundoora Repatriation Hospital in Melbourne, he started to experiment by injecting guinea pigs with urine from manic patients to see if this caused manic symptoms to develop. He used lithium to dissolve what he thought was the toxin (uric acid) so that this could be injected. Cade's hypothesis was not proven, but he noticed that the guinea pigs receiving the lithium solution became less energetic and slowed down. Cade suggested lithium could be used to treat mental illness and started to use it in a number of patients with mania, schizophrenia, and depression. He found that lithium had a remarkable effect upon mania but limited effects upon the other conditions. Acute symptoms of mania were effectively cured and indeed Cade gave lithium to his brother who had manic depression.

9. Media representations of Prozac.

Cade's work did not initially lead to major changes in the treatment of mania. It was only some years later when Mogens Schou, a Danish psychiatrist, undertook a scientific trial that confirmed Cade's observation that lithium calmed manic patients.

However, there was a further delay before lithium was officially approved for use in patients. This was partly because in the early days it was not clear what a therapeutic dose of lithium should be and too high a dose could lead to potentially fatal lithium toxicity. It was also true that there was little incentive for Pharma companies to produce lithium tablets as lithium was a naturally occurring substance, and so no drug company could patent it or realistically make any profit from it.

Nowadays, lithium is widely used, mainly for bipolar disorder, and it is a better anti-manic as compared to antidepressant drug. It is not uniformly the treatment of choice as a mood stabilizer as its prescription has to be accompanied by regular blood testing and monitoring to prevent toxicity. As such, it is more popular in some countries than others (e.g. it is more widely prescribed in Europe than the USA). Other medications that may stabilize cell membranes are also prescribed as mood stabilizers, including drugs initially introduced as anti-convulsants (e.g. sodium valproate).

From time to time the idea has been expressed that we should harness the potential effects of a natural salt such as lithium (see Box 7). The argument is that we could increase everyone's exposure to it with schemes akin to the prevention of tooth decay by fluoridation of water. Such calls often follow media articles such as the one in December 2009 when a report from a Japanese study in Oita suggested that suicide rates were lower in areas

Box 7 Lithium tonic

Lithium was marketed as a tonic in the 1920s.

Charles Leiper Grigg from the Howdy Corporation invented a tonic/hangover cure containing lithium citrate which he called 'Bib-Label Lithiated Lemon-Lime Soda'. The name was subsequently changed to 7 UP (although it no longer contains lithium)!

where the amount of lithium in tap water was higher—leading to suggestions that lithium should be put in the drinking water.

Psychotherapies: from Freudian theory to contemporary practice

Psychological interventions and the notion of talking being part of the therapeutic approach to asylum patients were described prior to the 1930s. However, it was Freud who clarified that talking with patients was not simply a vehicle for expressing empathy and support. He suggested that if the conversation was guided by an underlying psychological theory it could be used to bring about a talking cure. This was (and is) called psychoanalysis and, whilst current views on psychoanalysis are quite polarized, the introduction of a non-physical, non-drug treatment of depression represents one of the most important innovations. We briefly consider Freudian approaches and then discuss current psychotherapy interventions and some of the issues that may act as barriers to wider use of therapies.

Freud utilized his theories of the mind and ego defences and argued that it was important to target the symptoms that he believed represented unconscious conflicts. The therapy was often long with several sessions per week for many years. During therapy the patient lay on a couch while Freud sat behind the person's head and therefore out of their field of vision. The patient was encouraged to talk of anything that came to mind (a process Freud called free association) or to describe dreams. The therapist was trained to be 'like a blank canvas' onto which the patient could project issues from their past or could relive relationship conflicts. The therapist's skill was in making interpretations about what the patient said or did during therapy. Freud suggested that this process allowed the patient to gain understanding and insight into unconscious conflicts in their life that had generated the symptoms they were experiencing. Developing insight was believed to lead to resolution of symptoms and allow the patient to continue on a path of more healthy personal development.

Freud's critics point to multiple weaknesses in the model he proposed and it is easy to see that there are many flaws in this approach. However, it is worth remembering the era in which Freud began to practise psychoanalysis and a cursory glance at the rationale given and the nature of the physical treatments used would lead any reasonable observer to conclude that the latter interventions were equally defective. Perhaps a more telling observation is that most physical treatments have evolved more over time than psychoanalysis. Also, a valid criticism of psychoanalysis is that it risked being a rather exclusive club. Not only because most of the patients needed to be able to fund private therapy sessions several times a week for many years, but also because they needed to be able to express their emotions and difficulties in detail—perhaps indicating a certain level of income and education. This led to claims that the best candidates for these talking therapies were 'YARVIS' patients—young, articulate, rich, verbal, intelligent, and successful. Further concerns revolved around the notion that whilst the development of insight and self-awareness may be helpful it may not automatically promote change in how people act or cope.

Many of the current briefer interventions that are now available, such as counselling, interpersonal therapy (IPT), and cognitive behaviour therapy (CBT), are suitable for a broader group of depressed patients than Freudian analysis. Furthermore, interventions such as IPT and CBT extend beyond helping people understand their actions and reactions to include specific techniques that explicitly focus on changing behaviours and reducing the risk of future episodes of depression. These therapies also emphasize that the patient and therapist are collaborators in the process of change with a more equal relationship than that adopted in psychoanalysis (where the therapist is clearly in a position of power). Also, new therapies are evolving that combine elements of more than one therapy model, for example cognitive analytic therapy (CAT) combines some of the ideas of psychoanalysis and CBT.

Mindfulness represents a new mainstream therapy that is primarily a new take on meditation as practised in many religions throughout history. Mindfulness therapy encourages individuals to develop moment by moment awareness of bodily sensations, thoughts, feelings, and the environment. The therapy uses integrated relaxation and other interventions to help people take a non-judgemental approach towards their thoughts and feelings and to reduce their stress through acceptance and adaptation. If continued as a long-term habit it can prevent relapse, especially in those who had previously experienced repeated episodes of depression.

Media articles suggest that therapy is more popular than medication for the treatment of depression. However, enthusiasm for therapies in the public at large is not universal and research evidence suggests that about 30 per cent of patients do not want therapy or do not complete a course of therapy. Interestingly, this percentage is very similar to the rates of refusal or dropout from treatment with antidepressant medications. A barrier to the use of all therapies is that not everyone who is depressed wishes to engage in a talking treatment and also a desire to receive therapy does not guarantee that an individual will have a good outcome from this approach.

A further barrier to increasing access to therapies is the fact that some respected scientists and many scientific journals remain ambivalent about the empirical evidence for the benefits of psychological therapies. Part of the reticence appears to result from the lack of very large-scale clinical trials of therapies (compared to international, multi-centre studies of medication). However, a problem for therapy research is that there is no large-scale funding from big business for therapy trials, in contrast to Pharma funding for medication studies. Until funding is available to undertake long-term, multinational, multi-centre studies of therapies there will continue to be a delay in the accumulation of robust evidence about how best to employ therapies in clinical practice.

It is hard to implement optimum levels of quality control in research studies of therapies. A tablet can have the same ingredients and be prescribed in almost exactly the same way in different treatment centres and different countries. If a patient does not respond to this treatment, the first thing we can do is check if they receive the right medication in the correct dose for a sufficient period of time. This is much more difficult to achieve with psychotherapy and fuels concerns about how therapy is delivered and potential biases related to researcher allegiance (i.e. clinical centres that invent a therapy show better outcomes than those that did not) and generalizability (our ability to replicate the therapy model exactly in a different place with different therapists).

Some of the critiques of the evidence-base for therapies are far-fetched, but it is certainly true that at times the benefits, acceptability, and ease of delivering high-quality therapy have been overstated. It is also clear that there has been a lack of attention to side effects or adverse effects of therapies, and recent surveys, such as those carried out by Glynis Parry and colleagues in the United Kingdom, suggest that up to one in ten individuals report negative reactions to therapy.

Overall, the ease of prescribing a tablet, the more traditional evidence-base for the benefits of medication, and the lack of availability of trained therapists in some regions means that therapy still plays second fiddle to medications in the majority of treatment guidelines for depression.

Current treatment approaches

The mainstay of treatments offered to individuals with depression has changed little in the last thirty to forty years. Antidepressants are the first-line intervention recommended in most clinical guidelines, although it is increasingly recognized that brief therapies are an important option. Perhaps the most noticeable change in recent years is the shift away from the 'doctor knows best' approach towards a recognition that individuals have the right to express their treatment preferences and be involved in a process of shared decision-making. This shift is allied to the increased emphasis on personalized medicine, and the need to modify treatments to make them more relevant to each individual patient. As such, these issues will be briefly discussed.

Much of the treatment research in the 21st century focused on finding antidepressants that overcame the symptoms of an acute illness episode. It was stated that it takes about two weeks for medication to start to work, six weeks for people to feel significantly better, and that the medications should be continued for three to six months at least in an effort to minimize the risk of a relapse. This approach exposed three issues: first, individuals were not always good at sticking with a medication regime and not everyone completed a course of treatment. Second, medication only works for as long as an individual takes it; once it was stopped the risk of relapse rose significantly. Third, depression is a highly recurrent disorder and treating the acute episode is really only part of the equation, so treatment approaches needed to incorporate strategies to avoid further episodes as well. Clearly these problems needed to be addressed at a system level and at an individual level.

The increasing recognition that depression was a life course illness has led to several attempts to copy the systematic health services employed for chronic physical illnesses such as diabetes or hypertension. These chronic disease management models involve several key elements that are useful in helping people with depression, including an emphasis on long-term outcomes not just acute episodes; a greater expectation that primary care or community health services will provide a 'call and recall' system to ensure the service is more proactive in supporting and monitoring the person's progress and any barriers to treatment (and not just leaving everything up to the patient etc.); clearer treatment pathways (including how to decide to move to the next step in the treatment process); and shared care guidelines providing transparency about which individuals should be referred to specialist services and who can be best helped by primary care or other services.

Such systems of health care and treatment for depression have been implemented with varying degrees of success in different countries. The main benefits have been to help clinicians and individuals with depression to take a longer-term view of the problem and to offer a better method for deciding which treatments to use for different individuals. The down side is that the system is still not sufficiently sensitive to individual preferences and the personal differences that may critically influence treatment outcomes.

What makes one person with depression adhere to taking antidepressants for months or even years and another person to stop the medication after a few days? For years, the perceived wisdom was that it was side effects of medication. Although the newer antidepressants have different side effects from the earlier medications, the actual percentage of individuals who complete a course of treatment has remained the same for around fifty years (at about 60 per cent). Furthermore, studies suggest that about 5 per cent of non-adherers never took the prescription to be dispensed by a pharmacist (so they clearly could not have experienced any side effects). An alternative explanation of non-adherence with antidepressants was that individuals with severe depression perhaps lacked 'insight' into the need for treatment and so, it was argued, the illness impeded their awareness of what would help them and reduced their ability to adhere. However, this 60 per cent adherence rate is pretty similar to that reported for people with chronic physical illnesses who do not have any loss of insight. Lastly, it was argued that the individuals did not want medication, and wanted the option of therapy; but, as already noted, the refusal or dropout rate from therapies is similar to that reported for medication. So, the only conclusion we can draw is that individual differences are more likely to explain what is seen in the real world than some 'group experience' or herd instinct.

One of the best ways to understand the phenomenon described is to explore health belief models. In their simplest form these models explore how people understand and react to illness and what they think about treatments. Although the content of an individual's health beliefs may reflect their culture and background, there are five recurring themes that allow some predictions to be made about how a person will engage with different treatment approaches. The key questions that people think about in regard to their illness experiences are:

What is it?
What caused it?
Can it be cured or controlled?
What is the time-line?
What are the consequences?

To give a simple example, someone may believe that the problem they have is depression; that it is caused by a chemical imbalance in the brain; that it can be cured by taking a medication to correct that problem; and they may be worried that it may recur with negative effects on their social and work life. It is highly likely that this person will accept a prescription for an antidepressant and adhere to treatment for quite an extended period of time.

Someone who is not convinced that the problem is depression, who views their current state as indicative of personality weakness and believes that 'pulling themselves together' will resolve their problems once and for all, may be ambivalent about any sort of treatment. Alternatively, someone may agree that they have depression but may emphasize the role played by childhood trauma in undermining their self-esteem and describe that they know that they are very sensitive to feeling down in response to relationship stress. This individual may want help with their depression, but might decline medication (or question its utility), preferring instead to attend therapy.

The examples given are somewhat black and white, but they highlight that it is not just what treatment has been shown to work in a clinical treatment trial, but what treatment makes sense to any individual at the time they seek help. It goes without saying that the clinician has to strive to collaborate with a patient and take on board their perspective so that both parties can develop a shared understanding of the problem and make joint decisions about the course of action. This often requires a willingness by clinicians to modify their consulting style, and of course some find this more difficult than others. Interestingly, this philosophy is not as new as some individuals suggest; as long ago as 1878 a physician called William Osler reportedly said that 'The good clinician treats the disease; the great clinician treats the person.'

Chapter 6
Current controversies, future directions

Some people believe depression is massively over-diagnosed, some believe it to be an understandable reaction to life that should not be medicalized or treated, and some view depression as a diagnosable disorder, but disagree with the treatments that should be offered. We briefly explore these issues and then consider where the research on depression is heading in the next decade.

Is depression over-diagnosed?

Chapters 1 and 2 of this book identify remarkably consistent descriptions of depression in every type of recording that man has ever made. However, there are a few famous detractors, such as Thomas Szaz, who suggest it does not exist. At present, the major debate is not so focused on whether or not such an entity can be identified, but how depression has been classified or diagnosed, the professional and public attitudes to treatment, and the wildly varying theories about the causes. Ironically, research publications suggesting that depression is over-diagnosed and that too many prescriptions are given for antidepressants are matched closely by the number of papers highlighting that it is under-diagnosed and under-treated. Taken together these studies suggest that depression is frequently misdiagnosed and mistreated. For example, there is evidence that antidepressants are overused such as for individuals who have transient unhappiness or who have symptoms of depression that are not likely to benefit from medications. Also, at the other extreme, there is evidence that even if depression is recognized it may not be treated. For example, studies suggest that many elderly people with depression remain untreated because 'it is common to feel depressed if you have lots of physical ailments and you are getting older'. Such a rationale is difficult to fathom; clinicians understand that diabetes is common in older people, and they understand the causes, but this knowledge does not lead to treatment being withheld. However, experts in depression are aware that even if they improve the accuracy of the diagnosis of depression, questions remain about what the most appropriate treatment is for individuals with a disorder that may differ in its causes and its level of severity or complexity.

Do antidepressants work?

Since the introduction of tricyclic antidepressants there have been arguments about whether antidepressants work or not. For every review of published studies that state that they do work, there seem to be a similar number of reviews (often examining the same scientific publications) that state that they do not work any better than placebo (such as a sugar pill). However, in 2008 a storm broke in the news as a professor of psychology at Harvard Medical School called Irvine Kirsch published a new review that suggested that antidepressants were of very little benefit for treating depression. The big difference with this review compared to previous publications was that Kirsch and his colleagues used the Freedom of Information Act to get access to all the SSRI and new antidepressant drug trials submitted to the Food and Drug Administration (the organization responsible for licensing drugs in the USA). This meant that this new review included not only the studies that showed the drugs worked but also the studies that did not show any effect for antidepressants. The latter studies often remain unpublished and so were not available to many of the previous review articles.

As usual, it is not just the data included in Kirsch's review, but the interpretation of the findings that has contributed to the controversy. The basic scientific facts indicate that antidepressants can be beneficial to about 60–70 per cent of those who take them, but response to placebo may be around 30–50 per cent. So, in absolute terms about 20 per cent more people with depression will truly be better off because they took an antidepressant than if they did not. However, there are two important caveats about these findings. First, individuals with severe depression definitely benefit from antidepressants rather than placebo, but the benefits in mild and moderate depression are less clear. Some studies showed benefits for antidepressants in mild and moderate depression, but others showed no absolute improvement over and above that attained with placebo. Second, many of the studies were of very short duration and only examined benefits over about six weeks. Many experts suggest this undermines the validity of the review as this differs from how assessments are often made in day-to-day clinical settings, where these medications are often prescribed for longer and the response to treatment is often observed at a later time.

We would make four further observations about the prescribing and benefits of antidepressants. First, there has been significant progress in preventing drug companies from 'burying bad news' and in some instances data are now available online to allow independent researchers access to clinical trial information. This is an important step forward. Antidepressants are the second most commonly prescribed medications on the planet, their production is a multi-million pound industry, and the public and professionals need to be able to believe the information provided by the Pharma companies.

Second, before we write an obituary for second generation antidepressants it is worth noting than many medications prescribed for physical disorders, such as anti-inflammatory drugs, have never shown more than a 60–70 per cent response rate (versus the same 30–40 per cent placebo response rate). This means that just like antidepressants, treatments for physical disorders may only show the same 20 per cent absolute difference between the active medication and placebo treatments. However, the public have not stopped taking these medications for their physical illnesses and clinicians have not stopped prescribing them. What has happened is that prescribers have tried to target the use of medications towards those who can benefit from them.

Third, many cancer treatments are only effective for small subgroups of patients and many such improvements are short-lived (e.g. a group of patients with a certain type of tumour); it is unrealistic to expect a broad class of drugs such as antidepressants to work equally well for everyone or for every type of depression. Learning from specialities such as cancer, we need to be able to use different antidepressants or therapies more selectively and find possible predictors of which approach is best in different circumstances.

Fourth, whilst some cases of mild–moderate depression can benefit from antidepressants (e.g. chronic mild depression of several years' duration can often respond to medication), it is repeatedly shown that the only group who consistently benefit from antidepressants are those with severe depression. The problem is that in the real world, most antidepressants are actually prescribed for less severe cases, that is, the group least likely to benefit; which is part of the reason why the argument about whether antidepressants work is not going to go away any time soon.

Are all psychological therapies equally effective for depression?

There are debates within the therapy world about which approaches are most helpful for people who are depressed. For example, counselling may be useful in the short term, especially for individuals who lack social support or a confidant in the community. However, the benefits of counselling fade within 3–6 months of ending the sessions. So if the goal is longer-term gains and also prevention of future depressive episodes, therapies that explicitly aim to help people change how they act and cope may be preferred. The argument that individuals could simply repeat a course of counselling fails to take into account the fact that therapy sessions can be more costly in the short term than prescribing medication. The economic argument for therapy can only be sustained if it is shown that the long-term outcome of depression (fewer relapses and better quality of life) is improved by receiving therapy instead of medication or by receiving both therapy and medication.

Despite claims about how therapies such as CBT, behavioural activation, IPT, or family therapy may work, the reality is that many of the elements included in these therapies are the same as elements described in all the other effective therapies (sometimes referred to as empirically supported therapies). The shared elements include forming a positive working alliance with the depressed person, sharing the model and the plan for therapy with the patient from day one, and helping the patient engage in active problem-solving, etc. Given the degree of overlap, it is hard to make a real case for using one empirically supported therapy instead of another. Also, there are few predictors (besides symptom severity and personal preference) that consistently show who will respond to one of these therapies rather than to medication.

It also takes some time to establish that a therapy has short-term and long-term benefits across different patient groups (defined by age or type of mood disorder, etc.) and across countries and cultures. For example, despite the enthusiasm for mindfulness, there were fewer than twenty high-quality research trials on its use in adults with depression by the end of 2015 and most of these studies had fewer than 100 participants. So, whilst the signs are encouraging for the use of mindfulness, it is hard to argue the case to change international treatment guidelines on the basis of the examination of its use in 2,000 patients who mainly reside in Europe and the USA.

Complementary and alternative therapies

Depression is recognized as one of the most common reasons for seeking complementary or alternative therapies. Complementary medicine covers a wide range of therapies including herbal medicines and minerals as well as physical treatments such as acupuncture, reiki, and exercise, to name but a few.

Seeking alternatives may reflect dissatisfaction with conventional treatments in some individuals, whilst in others these approaches may be more in line with their health belief models or philosophy. For example, homoeopathy offers many individuals a more personalized level of input and explicitly attends to the whole person, which a person may feel is lacking in mainstream services. As noted, expectations of benefit from a treatment account for about 30 per cent of the response rate, and so the 'placebo effect' is relevant to any treatment whether provided by conventional or alternative services. However, in 2010 the House of Commons Science and Technology Committee in the United Kingdom concluded that there is no consistent or reliable evidence that homoeopathy is any more effective than a placebo and that the explanations of how or why homoeopathy could work are scientifically implausible. At the risk of upsetting some people we respect and admire, we concur with that report and find the so-called evidence in support of homoeopathy extremely hard to swallow.

One of the main reasons that many individuals support the use of herbal remedies is their beliefs that as these substances are naturally occurring they are by definition safe. Alas, this is not always true. One problem is that herbal remedies are not regulated or tested in the way that conventional drugs are and this can mean that two different over-the-counter preparations of the same remedy can have a twentyfold difference in their dose or potency or they may contain a range of additional substances. Secondly, many can have unwanted effects, the classic example being St John's Wort (SJW). This is an extract of the *Hypericum* plant and has been described as an antidepressant throughout history. Although the findings from clinical trials suggest the effect of SJW on depression is rather weak, it can benefit some individuals with milder levels of depression. However, the down side is that it interacts with the enzyme systems responsible for the metabolism of many other drugs (altering their blood concentrations and their efficacy), for example, it can render oral contraceptives less effective. Also, it can reduce absorption of iron into the body, increasing the risk of anaemia. Thus, enthusiasm for natural remedies must still be balanced by the recognition that few substances exist that are truly free from any side effects.

Perhaps the most promising alternative approach which is increasingly being adopted by mainstream clinical services is the prescription of exercise for some individuals with clinical depression. The benefits of exercise have been widely expounded for the population at large whether they have experienced depression or not. Indeed, public health campaigns are actively promoting the need to get people 'off the sofa' with slogans such as 'sitting is the new smoking'. Numerous studies demonstrate that exercise has health benefits that extend to psychological as well as physical well-being. However, this does not answer the question of whether regular exercise can reduce clinical depression. When the data from the best thirty studies are combined, the answer is a qualified 'yes'. The evidence is that exercise improves the symptoms of depression compared to no treatment at all, but the currently available studies on this topic are less than ideal (with many problems in the design of the study or sample of participants included in the clinical trial).

Exercise as the only treatment approach is probably most beneficial for those with milder forms of depression. This is not to suggest that other depressed individuals do not benefit, but rather that some severely depressed people may find it very hard to initiate a visit to a gym, let alone execute an exercise programme. These individuals may need medication in the first instance with opportunities to participate in exercise being offered after some improvement in symptoms has occurred. Exercise is likely to be a better option for those individuals whose mood improves from participating in the experience, rather than someone who is so depressed that they feel further undermined by the process or feel guilty about 'not trying hard enough' when they attend the programme.

There are several plausible arguments as to why exercise interventions may be beneficial, including the idea that psychologically, exercise will actively help to distract people from their negative thinking and ruminations, and that their self-esteem may be improved as they develop their skills and master particular activities; and socially, they may re-establish or improve their networks. Physiologically, as well as changing endorphin levels there is emerging evidence that exercise may produce changes in monoamine levels, or reduce levels of the cortisol. This means exercise could help to reverse some of the biological changes that have been found in people who become depressed.

Future developments in medications

As noted, there are gaps in the theoretical models of depression and some frustrations with the currently available medications to treat it. Like the rest of medicine, psychiatry continues to explore and revise the theories of how depression develops and how to identify individuals at risk for this condition. In the latter part of the 20th century, researchers established that there were connections between the systems already implicated in the development of depression; namely, that the monoamine and stress hormone systems were interconnected and, furthermore, there were bidirectional influences on the activity of these systems and genetic and psychological vulnerabilities, and environmental factors. At the start of this century, researchers have also turned their attention to the links of the monoamine system and HPA axis to the circadian and immune systems. Whilst a detailed discussion of each topic is beyond the scope of this book, we highlight a few key elements of this new research and highlight how it may help us discover much-needed new treatments.

Mood disorders and circadian rhythms

There is evidence that many individuals are larks and get up early every day, whilst others are night owls by nature. These sleep–wake patterns can also vary somewhat with age. Many of you will have seen with your own eyes that some adolescents have an amazing ability to sleep until well after lunch-time, to complain of still feeling tired all afternoon, and then to stay up well beyond midnight into the early hours of the next morning (suggesting their entire twenty-four-hour sleep–wake activity pattern is shifted). Also, you may personally have undertaken shift work or experienced jet lag following a long-haul aeroplane flight. The sleep–wake patterns exhibited by different individuals or by the same individual in different circumstances are partly explained by the activity of the circadian system or the internal body clock.

The term circadian derives from the Latin and means about (*circa*) one day (*diem*). Many processes in the body are carefully regulated by the rhythmic release of certain chemicals and hormones. The sleep—wake cycle is the most obvious example of this but blood pressure, body temperature, and many other biological functions change in a precise and regular pattern over the course of a day. Also, like an orchestra, the activity needs to be synchronized and disruptions to the sequence of hormone secretion or pattern of circadian activity can lead to significant changes in mood, sleep, concentration, appetite, and energy, giving a picture that looks very similar to clinical depression.

Disruptions of the circadian system are also implicated in the development in some people of medical problems such as obesity, diabetes, and some cancers; suggesting it has a role in physical and mental well-being.

There are several pieces of evidence that suggest a link between circadian abnormalities and mood disorders. First, genes (such as the so-called clock genes) play a role in setting each individual's internal biological clock and some types of clock genes are found more often than expected in families with a history of mood disorders such as depression and manic depression, and some of the clock genes that are present in individuals who develop mood disorders appear to exert weaker control over the system than in people who do not get depressed. Second, it is also known that circadian rhythms are very sensitive to environmental changes: the amount of daylight hours, social factors such as a regular lifestyle, and certain types of life events can significantly influence an individual's rhythms. Third, there are clear connections between the areas of the brain that regulate the circadian system and those that modulate the stress hormone and monoamine systems and many SSRIs and other antidepressants increase the levels of the main hormone involved in sleep regulation (called melatonin). Taken together, these findings have led many researchers to propose that abnormalities in an individual's biological clock may play a role in the development of mood disorders.

The findings described have stimulated interested in chronobiology (the study of cyclical physiological phenomena) and many studies are now being undertaken of the variation in daytime activity and night-time sleep patterns of people with mood disorders. This research is aided by the fact that it is possible for people to wear an actiwatch (a device that looks similar to an ordinary watch and can be worn on the wrist that measures motion) twenty-four hours a day, seven days a week, and carry on with their normal life. This means it is possible to record naturalistic or real world information about their patterns and routines. These so-called ecological studies demonstrate that individuals at risk of developing mood disorders (such as those with a strong family history), those with a current episode of depression, and those with a past history of depression (but who are currently well) all show differences in their sleep pattern from individuals with none of these characteristics. It has also been shown that disturbed sleep predicts worsening of mood, concentration, rumination, and lowered activity on the following day, and that improving sleep can help reverse these trends.

The research on circadian rhythms has increased interest in chronobiotics (drugs that may affect the circadian system) and chronotherapeutics (interventions such as light therapy and CBT for insomnia: CBT-I). Currently, there are major research trials of the treatment of depression examining the benefits of melatonin or synthetic compounds that mimic the effects of melatonin. Therapies used to treat insomnia, such as CBT-I, have also been adapted for use in bipolar disorders and web-based internet programmes are being used to modify the sleep-activity patterns of young people with emerging mood disorders. Studies of light therapy, using light boxes and specially designed glasses that block out blue light, are under way in individuals with depression, bipolar disorder, and in individuals who have seasonal affective disorder (mood disturbances that change according to the season). All of these approaches appear to be opening up much needed avenues for new treatments.

Depression and the immune system

Depression is not an infectious disease, but it seems that some proteins in our body, called inflammatory markers, are increased in individuals with acute episodes of depression and in children who later develop depression in adolescence. Inflammatory factors have been found to affect various activities of the brain thought to be important in depression, including altering monoamine activity, cortisol receptor responses, and the neuroplasticity of the hippocampus (neuroplasticity refers to the brain's ability to form new neural connections). Professor Peter Jones and researchers from the University of Cambridge have suggested that early life adversity and stress can lead individuals to develop persistent increases in the levels of inflammatory markers in the body. Furthermore, individuals with persistently higher levels of inflammatory markers or those who show an excessive inflammatory response to stress are about twice as likely to get depressed as those with low levels of markers.

Even when we are healthy there will be some traces of inflammatory markers in the bloodstream (especially substances such as interleukin-6). However, when we have an infection, such as a common cold, our immune system kicks into action to fight the infection and inflammatory markers are released. These substances also act on the brain and produce 'sickness behaviours' (nausea, fever, loss of appetite, withdrawal from the physical and social environment), many of which overlap with the symptoms of depression. The difference between sickness-related behaviour and depression is that the former is the body's adaptive response to the infection and the behaviour and symptoms stop once the infection is resolved. This is not always the case in depression and high levels of inflammatory markers can be more common in those who experience prolonged episodes of depression.

As with the circadian system, immune system abnormalities are linked to both mental and physical disorder. For example, we know that people with depression have a higher risk of developing heart disease and diabetes, and it has been shown that elevated levels of inflammatory markers increase the risk of these problems in the general population. A goal of future research is to establish whether immune or circadian abnormalities explain the association between mood disorders and specific physical health problems. An additional reason for interest in the immune system and circadian markers is that they can be measured objectively and so they may eventually allow researchers to develop laboratory tests similar to those used routinely in general medicine to help identify people at risk of a particular illness or to decide the best treatment options.

Future research in psychotherapy and the links to neuroscience

One of the reasons for some scepticism about the value of therapies for treating depression is that it has proved difficult to demonstrate exactly what mediates the benefits of these interventions. This has led many to claim that the improvements seen are akin to the placebo effect or are simply a consequence of having someone to confide in who provides support during a difficult time. However, it is also clear that the therapies that are most beneficial for depression help people change their thinking, emotional reactions, and behaviours, especially in response to life stress. This suggests that effective therapies include learning new skills such as changing a person's coping strategies and revising their self-perceptions of stressors. As such, therapy researchers have started to combine psychological, social, and neuroscience approaches in their studies to explore the underlying brain activities related to depression and how these change during therapy and after recovery.

One of the best-known advocates of this research strategy is Eric Kandel, who won a Nobel Prize for his laboratory research on the physiological basis of learning and memory in 2000. What makes his contribution so fascinating is that although he is well known as a basic scientist, he originally trained as a psychoanalyst. Kandel has continued to emphasize the importance of understanding that what we call the mind can be understood as the activity of the brain and that all mental processes, even the most complex, derive from operations of the brain. Kandel is not the only academic to discuss these issues, but he has clearly articulated how neuroscience, and especially the use of brain imaging techniques, could allow researchers to develop new ways for exploring mental processes, of identifying the brain changes that may occur in depression and also examining how these may be modified by antidepressants or psychological treatments. This type of approach is critical to attempts to uncover the connections between specific mental functions and specific brain mechanisms, but also the links to genetics, biology, and psychosocial models.

In 2008, Kandel published a paper on a new intellectual framework for psychiatry. He argued that research repeatedly demonstrates that genetic influences are not fixed (i.e. the old notion that you inherit a behaviour pattern that cannot be changed is wrong), and that we know that internal stimuli (events within the body) and external events are involved in the development of the brain, such as stress, learning, and social interactions. Importantly, all these events can alter 'gene expression' (which is termed epigenetic regulation). When learning and experience produce these alterations in gene expression this in turn affects the patterns of neuronal connections and leads to anatomical changes in the brain; a process that can continue throughout life.

A simple example of this brain plasticity comes from the frequently quoted study of London taxi drivers. During their probation period, would-be taxi drivers have to learn a detailed roadmap of London (known as *The Knowledge*), which may take four to five years to achieve. Researchers used brain scans to demonstrate that these navigational demands stimulated brain development and it was found that the individuals learning *The Knowledge* showed an increase in the size of the hippocampus in the brain. Further, the scans showed that their intensive training was responsible for the growth in their memory centre (i.e. it was not that individuals who already had a large hippocampus were more likely to decide to become taxi drivers). In clinical studies, it has been shown that normal development of the cortex (the large lobes of the brain) may be retarded by exposure to neglect or deprivation in early life and that the effects of this include reduced modulation of other brain areas involved in emotional reactivity, fear, and responses to danger (areas called the limbic, midbrain, and brain stem regions).

These studies are important to depression and to psychotherapy research in a number of ways. First, in depression it is likely that certain life experiences lead to the growth (or retraction) of neural networks in the brain that are then reactivated under stress. As the researcher Carla Schatz stated, this can be described as 'cells that fire together wire together'. This model provides a potential neural basis to cognitive structures such as our underlying beliefs and our ability to regulate emotions. Also, it offers insights into neuroplasticity and the investigation of the substances in the brain, such as the protein called brain-derived neurotrophic factor (BDNF), that stimulate the growth of new nerve cells and improve their healthy functioning and survival time. Interestingly, research reports increased BDNF levels can be associated with repeated exercise, therapy, or taking medication.

Kandel argues that psychological interventions can produce long-term changes in behaviour through learning, which in turn produces changes in gene expression, and therefore alters the strength of connections between nerve synapses and brings about structural changes in the brain. The race is now on to try to use new technology to determine if he is right and to examine whether therapy works in this way and, if so, where the therapy-induced changes occur (see Figure 10). Researchers are also trying to examine whether the structural reorganization produced by therapy occurs in the same parts of the brain that are altered by the depression itself, or in different brain regions (which would suggest that therapy produced compensatory changes). Lastly, researchers are comparing the brain scans of individuals receiving therapy or medications to determine whether the effects on the brain are similar or different.

The research so far has produced interesting but inconsistent results. For example, a Finnish study demonstrated that depression

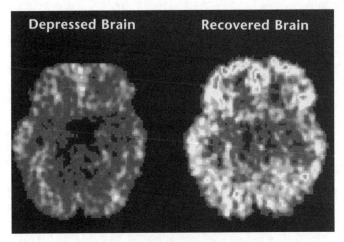

10. Understanding the mind and brain. This brain scan (using positron emission tomography or PET) provides a window to view the activity of the brain of a person with depression before and after receiving sixteen sessions of therapy. The image on the left shows the brain of the person when they were depressed and the scan on the right shows the brain of that person after successful treatment.

was associated with reduced serotonin uptake in some frontal areas of the brain and that this abnormality was corrected in patients who received a course of therapy, but did not change in patients who did not receive treatment. North American research has indicated that the changes in brain activity following a course of CBT and IPT were similar to each other (suggesting they may have comparable effects on similar brain areas), but differed from the effects of antidepressants. In some CBT studies, changes have been found in blood flow in parts of the frontal lobes associated with the appraisal of emotions and ideas, which have been interpreted as a possible indication that the person is ruminating less as they recover from their depression. This research is in its infancy and it will take some time to be confident about the interpretation of the findings. However, this scientific approach holds out the prospects of being able to identify which individuals will respond to which type of treatment for depression and also to show how the use of antidepressants or therapy can produce changes in the brain that lead to recovery from depression. Not surprisingly, this has caught the attention of many parts of the scientific community working in psychiatry, psychology, general medicine, and neuroscience.

Chapter 7
Depression in modern society

No age, gender, or social group is immune to depression and even when strict criteria are used to define clinical depression it is still a very common human experience. As such it is worthwhile considering the global impact of depression and how major international bodies such as the World Health Organization and World Bank have tried to estimate the real world impact of depression and the economic costs to society. The findings from this work are starting to influence government policies in many countries, as well as encouraging more proactive attempts to tackle depression internationally. Also, this has fostered new thinking on the problem of depression in the workforce, introducing concepts such as 'mental capital'. One reason that members of the workforce may be reluctant to seek help is because of the stigma associated with depression and it is useful to consider how this may undermine a person's willingness to access treatment and the lessons to be learned from campaigns that have tried to combat prejudice. Finally, we briefly examine the notion of genius and madness and whether there is any evidence for an association between creativity and mood disorders.

Measuring the global burden of disease

For many decades, the most common measure of the health status of a population was the rate of deaths per 1,000 individuals within a defined area (such as a region or country). However, from the 1980s onwards, it became increasingly obvious that mortality rates are not the most useful way to capture the true extent of the individual, personal, and economic burden that a particular illness places on society. For example, some disorders, although not immediately leading to death, might impair the day-to-day functioning of large numbers of individuals over many years, preventing them from participating in the job market. Also, their illness might significantly impact on family members who then have to take time off from their own employment in order to provide care and support. For this reason, the World Health Organization and World Bank jointly commissioned The Global Burden of Disease Study. The goal of this project was to make a more meaningful assessment of the burden on individuals and society associated with a range of physical and mental disorders and a new measure of health status was created, the Disability Adjusted Life Year (DALY). The idea was that DALYs would reflect the combined effects of the years of health that are lost due to the morbidity (a measure of the ongoing disability connected to a disorder) as well as the mortality (measured by the number of premature deaths) associated with a particular illness in a given population. The work has become extremely well known and publications by the research group have been widely quoted, including one by Murray and Lopez (listed in 'References and further reading'). The latter publication is especially important because it demonstrated that the health problems placing the greatest burdens on society worldwide are substantially different from the leading causes of death.

Across all regions of the world, six mental health problems were ranked in the top ten most burdensome disorders and together they accounted for 28 per cent of DALYs for all physical and mental disorders across all age groups. As shown in Box 8, when the assessment of burden is restricted only to adults aged 19–45 years living in the developed world (which comprises 75 per cent of the world population), depression was ranked number one,

Box 8 The ten leading causes of global burden of disease in adults aged 19–45 years

	Total Disability Adjusted Life Years (DALYs) in millions	% of Total DALYs
All Causes	472.7	
Unipolar major depression	50.8	10.7
Iron deficiency anaemia	22.0	4.7
Falls	22.0	4.6
Alcohol use	15.8	3.3
Chronic respiratory disorders	14.7	3.1
Bipolar disorders	14.1	3.0
Birth abnormalities	13.5	2.9
Osteoarthritis	13.3	2.8
Schizophrenia	12.1	2.6
Obsessive compulsive disorders	10.2	2.2

(Adapted from *The Global Burden of Disease* by Murray and Lopez, 1996)

above all other physical and mental disorders (and bipolar disorders ranked sixth). Furthermore, depression was the most important contributor to DALYs in all world regions except Sub-Saharan Africa.

The study also explored how the patterns of the burden associated with different disorders would change in the future. One of the amazing findings was that—as we begin to eradicate problems that claim the lives of children in Africa such as malaria—more and more people will survive into early adulthood, which means more and more people are alive at the peak age of onset of depression and bipolar disorders. As such, the prediction for 2020 is that the DALYs lost to depression will rise even further, to 15 per cent of the overall total, placing depression second only to heart disease in terms of worldwide ranking for global disease burden for all age groups across all continents. Furthermore, a recent publication in *The Lancet*, led by a researcher named Gore, has already indicated that depression is the most burdensome condition worldwide in young people aged less than 25 years (with bipolar disorders ranked fourth).

The reason for examining this information in detail is to emphasize the staggering scale of the impact of depression and also to try to counter any lingering misperception that depression represents a minor ailment or some sort of personality flaw that can be easily dismissed. For far too long depression has been referred to as the 'common cold of psychiatry'. The Global Burden of Disease study demonstrates that this analogy fails to reflect the reality of the experience of depression in the modern world and is dangerously naive. It is true that, like the common cold, depression is highly prevalent; however, unlike the common cold, depression is not a mild or self-limiting disorder that will somehow disappear from society if we ignore it.

The economics of depression: depression in the workplace

Research has demonstrated that employment may have a protective role against the development of depression in many people, whilst unemployment or socio-economic deprivation may be stress factors that increase rates of depression in others. However, this does not mean that full employment will prevent everyone from getting depressed and international reports highlight that depression can be a significant problem in any workforce. In the United Kingdom, at the turn of this century, the Health and Safety Executive estimated that the number of workdays lost by individuals reporting depression was about twenty-two days per year and that this exceeded the days lost by individuals with other mental or physical disorders (who lost an average of 4–6 workdays per year). Research also indicates that treatment is important and a study from the USA in 2005 showed that those who took the prescribed antidepressant medications had a 20 per cent lower rate of absenteeism than those who did not receive treatment for their depression.

Absence from work is only one half of the depression–employment equation. In recent times, a new concept 'presenteeism' has been introduced to try to describe the problem of individuals who are attending their place of work but have reduced efficiency (usually because their functioning is impaired by illness). As might be imagined, presenteeism is a common issue in depression and a study in the USA in 2007 estimated that a depressed person will lose 5–8 hours of productive work every week because the symptoms they experience directly or indirectly impair their ability to complete work-related tasks. For example, depression was associated with reduced productivity (due to lack of concentration, slowed physical and mental functioning, loss of confidence), and impaired social functioning (due to social withdrawal and reduced ability to communicate).

Tensions and problems may arise at work, particularly if colleagues do not understand that the depressed person is under-functioning because of ill health rather than 'not pulling their weight'. Of course this can sometimes lead to a downward spiral because the depressed individual might not be able to retain their current employment, which can further damage their self-confidence and self-esteem. Not only can this reduce their chances of finding a new job, it can act as a further stress factor in their life and increase the chances that depression will persist or recur. A study from the USA in 2010 reported that individuals with depression are likely to have a 20 per cent reduction in their earning potential and are seven times more likely than the general population to be unemployed; a situation that worsens during economic downturns. According to the Mental Health Economics European Network, depression is the leading cause of long-term disability and early retirement.

Economic cost

In understanding the cost of depression, it is important to realize that the size of the economic burden will depend on how we set the boundaries for defining clinical depression and also what costs are included in the calculation.

The health care costs of treating clinical depression are frequently far greater than for other mental or chronic physical disorders. One of the first studies to compare the costs for different illnesses was undertaken in the England and Wales NHS in 1996. The cost of treating clinical depression was estimated at £887 million which exceeded the combined cost of treating both hypertension (£439 million) and diabetes (£300 million). A more recent Europe-wide study of 466 million people in 28 countries in 2013 demonstrated that depression was the most costly brain disorder in Europe (accounting for 33 per cent of costs for all disorders). The study estimated that at least 21 million Europeans were affected by depression at a total annual cost of €118 billion (corresponding to about €275 per inhabitant).

Health economists do not usually restrict their estimates of the cost of a disorder simply to the funds needed for treatment (i.e. the direct health and social care costs). A comprehensive economic assessment also takes into account the indirect costs. In depression these will include costs associated with employment issues (e.g. absenteeism and presenteeism; sickness benefits), costs incurred by the patient's family or significant others (e.g. associated with time away from work to care for someone), and costs arising from premature death such as depression-related suicides (so-called mortality costs). When these aspects are all

taken into account, a study in the USA in the year 2000
demonstrated that the total costs of depression were about
$83 billion each year; a sum that exceeds the costs of the war in
Afghanistan from 2001 until 2012.

Studies from around the world consistently demonstrate that the
direct health care costs of depression are dwarfed by the indirect
costs. For example, out of the $83 billion costs of depression in the
USA study, treatment costs constituted less than a third of the
total ($26 billion). A study of depression in England in 2005
showed that whilst the total health service costs over six months
were about £425 per person, the indirect costs averaged £2,575
per person. Interestingly, absenteeism is usually estimated to be
about one-quarter of the costs of presenteeism. For example, in
the USA in 2007, the cost of lost productivity due to absenteeism
in workers with depression was about $8.3 billion compared to
$35.7 billion due to presenteeism. In total, the economic
consequences of depression are estimated to be at least 1 per cent
of the GDP of Europe.

Mental health and wealth: the concept of mental capital

In the last thirty years, many societies have shifted towards
more knowledge- and service-based economies. A number of
international groups such as the Foresight government think
tank in the United Kingdom and the Trimbos Institute in the
Netherlands that have published reports comment that people
increasingly work with their heads rather than their hands. The
Foresight Report drew attention to the importance of developing
both mental capital and mental well-being in the wider population
as well as the possible threats posed by changes in working
practices that will occur over the next twenty years (see Box 9).
For example, the report identified that rates of depression might
increase in some individuals because they have difficulties in
adapting to new employment demands. The report concluded that

Box 9 What is mental capital?

According to the *Foresight Report* in the United Kingdom, the term mental capital refers to a person's cognitive and emotional resources. It combines

- their general abilities and how flexible and efficient they are at learning,
- their 'emotional intelligence', such as social skills and how resilient they are under stress.

It gives a snapshot of how well an individual is able to contribute effectively to society, and also to experience a high personal quality of life.

The report stated that:

the idea of mental capital naturally sparks associations with ideas of financial capital and it is both challenging and natural to think of the mind in this way.

how a nation develops its mental capital affects its economic competitiveness and prosperity and its mental well-being, social cohesion, and inclusion. Given that depression is the biggest cause of absenteeism and presenteeism, the work on mental capital extends interest in the global impact of depression beyond its economic cost to its economic significance.

In her thesis on mental capital, the Dutch academic Rifka Weehuizen comments that whilst in the past, physical health was crucial for performance at a job, today, it is mental health. Also, she draws attention to evidence that new types of working practice and the pressure to be ever more productive may actually lead to higher levels of stress and depression and argues that this may explain the 'happiness paradox' where increasing numbers of individuals in the leading economies worldwide appear to be more unhappy despite being better off than their predecessors.

Weehuizen points out that what drives economic growth is not necessarily good for mental health, but mental health is essential for further growth.

Work in the United Kingdom, the Netherlands, and elsewhere emphasizes the need for governments to develop policies to maximize mental capital and to engage in mental health promotion. It also advocates the need for private and public investment in the mental health of the workforce. This has led to several initiatives such as workplace screening programmes to try to and detect depression and schemes offering 'in-house' counselling and treatment services. Some initiatives have also been developed to try to raise awareness of depression. These have attempted to increase the uptake of treatment by individuals with depression, but also to increase the knowledge of senior managers about the nature of the problem in the hope of making it easier for individuals to discuss depression without fear of prejudice or stigmatization.

In 2005 in the United Kingdom, Lord Layard, a renowned economist, published *The Depression Report* which specifically used data about the economic costs and economic significance of depression to successfully argue for investment in the treatment of depression and anxiety to try to reduce the long-term economic burden. Layard estimated that the cost of providing psychological therapies to individuals with depression would be entirely offset by the savings accrued by the Department of Work and Pensions as a result of reduced incapacity benefits payments and gains made by the Exchequer through increased tax revenues (as individuals returned to employment after treatment). He provided data to show that the incapacity benefit paid to an individual with anxiety or depression during the course of one month equated to the cost of providing them with about ten sessions of CBT (estimated at about £750). Although some of the assumptions he employed in making the calculations have been questioned, Layard's arguments proved to be persuasive and, on the basis of the programme being 'cost-neutral', up to 10,000 new therapists have been trained and hired to treat patients with depression and anxiety in primary care in the United Kingdom.

Stigma and depression

One of the by-products of the increasing understanding of the economic cost and global significance of depression is an emerging commitment to providing early treatment. Sadly, history tells us that depression often remains a 'hidden disability', because people fear the consequences of disclosure to their employer. For example, in 2009, a survey in the United Kingdom by the Time to Change organization (a group trying to combat stigma) revealed that 92 per cent of the public believed that admitting to having a mental health problem such as depression would damage someone's career. A study in the USA in 2005 produced similar findings and showed that 25 per cent of people with depression believed that admitting to being depressed also had a negative effect on their friendships.

Fear of rejection by work colleagues or friends is compounded by the fact that many people with depression also believe they will be stigmatized by the health care system. In this century, Anthony Jorm and his colleagues in Australia have repeatedly shown that a major barrier to help-seeking is that individuals with depression feel embarrassed and ashamed to talk about their problems with health professionals and also believe that many professionals will react negatively to them. Similar findings are reported around the globe.

A study in China in 2010 suggested that the overwhelming majority of depressed patients presenting to primary care talked only about their physical symptoms. The researchers commented that the Chinese patients probably suppressed or disguised their psychological problems because of their fear of the powerful stigma attached to depression in their culture. One of the potential consequences of the reluctance of depressed people to present to clinical services or to downplay the mental health elements of their problem is illustrated vividly in the Layard report. This identified that in people with long-term depression (even when the symptoms prevented them from working) less than 50 per cent were receiving effective treatments. Again, this finding has been replicated for cases of depression in the developing as well as in the developed world.

Numerous studies confirm that there is still a social stigma associated with depression. According to the English social psychiatrist Graham Thornicroft, to tackle stigma we need to consider its three key elements, namely: problems of knowledge (ignorance), problems of attitudes (prejudice), and problems of behaviour (discrimination). There have been a number of national campaigns such as 'Defeat Depression' in the United Kingdom, 'beyondblue' in Australia, and 'Depression Awareness, Recognition and Treatment' (DART) in the USA. The programmes all combined attempts to raise awareness in the general public alongside interventions targeting clinicians. Beyondblue also developed an internet website to educate young people about depression and to provide advice about how to access help.

In New Zealand, before embarking on a national campaign of their own, the Ministry of Health carried out a fascinating review of what had or had not proved effective in such campaigns elsewhere. Their report highlights that an 11 per cent improvement in depressive symptoms can be achieved through depression prevention programmes. The benefits of engaging with the media (such as the popular press and television) were more difficult to assess, but it was noted that advertisements featuring high-profile sportsmen and women or well-known celebrities who talked about their experiences of depression did produce some shifts in public attitudes (although this was not found in all countries). The document provided useful insights into the most important elements of a successful anti-stigma campaign (see Box 10).

Box 10 A review of depression campaigns undertaken to inform a public health campaign in New Zealand in 2005

A review of the evidence about how people change their health attitudes and behaviours, and which behaviours lead to better depression outcomes, identified the following knowledge, beliefs, and attitudes that relate to the motivation to act on depression:

- Knowledge of depression symptoms
- Knowledge of risk factors for depression that can be modified
- Confidence in help-seeking
- Knowledge of and attitudes towards health professionals (and their roles)
- Knowledge of and attitudes towards self-help and effective treatments
- Family and friends' knowledge of and attitudes to self-help, help-seeking, and treatments
- Society attitudes to depression.

The final issue to consider when examining how stigma may affect a person with depression is to also realize that having a depressive episode does not prevent a person from holding negative views about depression that reflect those of their community, culture, or the population at large. Prior to experiencing depression, a person may believe that depression is a sign of personal weakness, etc. This can fuel self-prejudice and lead the person to feel ashamed, to avoid acknowledgement of their problem, and to reject offers of potentially beneficial treatments.

Depression and creativity

The possible link between depression and creativity has been discussed since ancient times and in the 4th century BC Aristotle is said to have commented, 'Why is it that all men who are outstanding in philosophy, poetry or the arts are melancholics?' In modern times, Kay Jamison, an eminent researcher in the field of mood disorders, has written extensively on this topic and has published a book entitled *Touched with Fire*. Notably, Jamison makes the point that although some people romanticize and exaggerate the links between artists, composers, or writers and mood disorders, it would be wrong to dismiss out of hand this potentially positive aspect of mental disorders.

The roll call of creative artists throughout history who are reported to have experienced periods of depression or bipolar disorders is long and impressive. For example, poets and writers include William Blake, Lord Byron, John Keats, Robert Lowell, Sylvia Plath, Edgar Allan Poe, Mary Shelley, Robert Louis Stevenson, Leo Tolstoy, Mark Twain, and Virginia Woolf; artists include Michelangelo, Edvard Munch, Georgia O'Keeffe, Vincent van Gogh; and musicians range from Mozart, Handel, and Schumann to Charlie Mingus. The possible links between creativity and mood disorders have led a number of researchers to try to study the links, such as Joseph Schildkraut of Harvard, who tried to piece together the personal histories of mental health problems in a group of American painters known as the New York School of Abstract Expressionists. The study, called *Creativity's Melancholy Canvas*, was published in the *American Journal of Psychiatry* and showed that between six and eight of the fifteen artists probably had a history of depression or manic depression. Some also used drugs or drank alcohol to excess at the same time. Also, four of the group died prematurely. Gorky and Rothko committed suicide, whilst Jackson Pollock and David Smith died whilst driving cars recklessly (which some observers hypothesized might indicate suicidal intent).

Small-scale studies, whilst intriguing, do not offer proof of a robust link between creativity and depression. To do a scientific study of the association between creativity and depression, we would first need to define creativity (e.g. the dictionary refers to 'creative ability, resulting from originality of thought or expression'). We would then have to find a way to select a sample of creative people, and to use established criteria for recognizing depression or bipolar disorders in order to assess what proportion of the creative sample had experienced a mood disorder. Finally, to truly understand whether the rates of mood disorder are increased in our creative sample, we would also need to recruit a control group. For example, members of the general population who are not regarded as creative (but who ideally have the same average age, similar educational experiences, and show the same gender distribution as the creative group). Interestingly, there are published studies that apply some of these methods and try to answer the question 'do mood disorders occur in creative people more often than we would expect by chance?'

Two of the best-known studies on creativity and mood disorders were undertaken in the USA by Nancy Andreasen in the 1980s and Arnold Ludwig in the 1990s. Andreasen studied thirty writers (both male and female) and thirty control subjects (matched according to age and gender). Ludwig's study compared fifty-nine female writers (who were all attending the same conference) and fifty-nine female 'non-writers' in a matched control group. Although the size of these two studies is relatively small, they both showed that about 20–50 per cent of the writers surveyed had some form of mood disorder. Furthermore, depression was three times more likely and bipolar disorders were four times more likely to occur in writers than in the comparison groups. Andreasen also noted that the families of the writers had more relatives who were creative and had a history of mood disorders.

What we do not learn from these studies is whether the same factors that may make some people vulnerable to developing a mood disorder also predict that a person will be more creative than the average person. To explore this scientists have tried to determine what the most likely components are that would enable someone to be more creative and then to see if these are also characteristics of people who experience mood disorders. According to Goodwin and Jamison's textbook on *Manic-Depressive Illness*, the most common overlapping factors found in creativity and mood disorders are temperament (or personality style), thinking style (cognitive factors), and cyclical changes in mood. For example, when someone is hypomanic, their thinking may be speeded up and they may start to make more frequent and far-reaching links between different ideas, they may show a degree of disinhibition (meaning they may become more aware of things in their environment), and they have more energy and less need for sleep. All these things occurring together could allow someone to achieve a higher level of creativity than other people. Whilst it is easy to see how the experience of hypomania could facilitate creativity, it is less clear how the experience of depression can be helpful and it is widely reported that some literary figures, such as Virginia Woolf, were unable to write when they were depressed. Interestingly, this does not appear to be a universal experience and one survey of writers reported that 30 per cent noted that their mood actually worsened in the time immediately preceding a period of increased creativity. What most artists and writers seemed to acknowledge is that it is the depth and intensity of their feelings and moods that are important in helping them extend their creativity beyond their innate level. As Kay Jamison observes, it seems that the experience of depression or hypomania 'can allow for certain insights or changes in energy levels that may further enhance the creativity of naturally creative people'.

The next issue to consider is whether more severe episodes of mood disorders are associated with more creativity or if they render people unable to express their creativity. Sadly, writings over many centuries suggest that the latter is more often the case. For example, even during the Renaissance, there was a distinction made between 'sane melancholics' who were high achievers and those with an insanity that prevented them using their creative talents. It seems that when people are severely depressed their physical and mental activity may be so slowed down that they are unable to write, paint, or compose, In contrast, a severe manic episode may render an individual so chaotic that their creative ideas are so disorganized as to be incomprehensible.

The information we have described may mean that moderate but not extreme periods of mood disturbance can facilitate the creative process. As such, it is also important to try to determine if treatment is a help or a hindrance to creative people. A study of Irish and British writers by Kay Jamison found that a significant number had been treated for their mood problems and that more had been to therapy than taken medication. This tends to support the notion that writers and artists worry that medications may impair the creative process. To examine this, Morgen Schou (a psychiatrist who is famous for his influential role in introducing lithium into day-to-day treatment) undertook a small study of twenty-four artists and writers and compared their creative output before and after they were prescribed lithium in the late 1970s. His study found that twelve individuals (50 per cent) actually reported increased productivity, whilst a further six individuals reported no change. The other six individuals (25 per cent) reported that lithium treatment decreased their creativity to the extent that four of them declined to carry on taking it. Obviously, such a small study cannot provide a definitive answer, but it is interesting that treatment did not undermine the creative processes of the majority.

To summarize what is known to date, we can say that the majority of people with a mood disorder are not more creative than their peers. Furthermore, most creative people do not have a mood disorder. However, in those creative individuals who do have mood disorders, some of the symptoms of the disorder, such as intense emotional states and changes in thinking processes, may raise their creativity to a new level. We will leave you to decide whether Figure 11 is an accurate representation of what treatment has to offer these individuals.

"More lithium."

11. More lithium.

References and further reading

Chapter 1: A very short history of melancholia

Berrios, G. E. 2004. *A History of Mental Symptoms*. Cambridge: Cambridge University Press.

Jackson, S. W. 1986. *Melancholia and Depression; From Hippocratic Times to Modern Times*. New Haven: Yale University Press.

Redden, J. 2000. *The Nature of Melancholy: From Aristotle to Kristeva*. Oxford: Oxford University Press.

Chapter 2: The modern era: Diagnosis and classification of depression

Goodwin, F. K., and Jamison, K. R. 2007. *Manic Depressive Illness and Recurrent Depression*. 2nd edition. Oxford: Oxford University Press.

Porter, R. 1987. *Mind-Forg'd Manacles: A History of Madness in England from the Restoration to the Regency*. Cambridge, Mass.: Harvard University Press.

Storr, A. 1989. *Freud: A Very Short Introduction*. Oxford: Oxford University Press.

Chapter 3: Who is at risk of depression?

Goldberg, D. 2010. The detection and treatment of depression in the physically ill. *World Psychiatry*, 9: 16–20.

Marland, H. 2003. Disappointment and desolation: women, doctors and interpretations of puerperal insanity in the nineteenth century. *History of Psychiatry*, 14: 303–20.

WHO Health Evidence Network (HEN) Report. 2012. *For Which Strategies of Suicide Prevention is there Evidence of Effectiveness?* Copenhagen: World Health Organization.

Chapter 4: Models of depression

Beck, A. T., 1979. *Cognitive Therapy and the Emotional Disorders*. London: Penguin Books.

Brown, G. W., and Harris, T. O. 1978. *Social Origins of Depression: A Study of Psychiatric Disorder in Women*. London: Tavistock Publications.

Caspi, A. 2003. The influence of life stress on depression. *Science*, 301/5631: 386–9.

Crawford, M., Thana, L., Farquharson, L., Palmer, L., Hancock, E., Bassett, P., Clarke, J., and Parry, G. 2016. Patient experience of negative effects of psychological treatment: results of a national survey. *British Journal of Psychiatry*, 208: 260–5.

Hirschfeld, R. M. 2000. History and evolution of the monoamine hypothesis of depression. *Journal of Clinical Psychiatry*, 61, Suppl. 6: 4–6.

Maniam, J., Antoniadis, C., and Morris, M. 2014. Early-life stress, HPA axis adaptation, and mechanisms contributing to later health outcomes. *Frontiers in Endocrinology*, 5: 73.

Chapter 5: The evolution of treatments

Cade, J. 1949. Lithium salts in the treatment of psychotic excitement. *Medical Journal of Australia*, 2: 349–52.

Lopez-Munoz, F., and Alamo, C. 2009. Monoaminegic neurotransmission: the history of the discovery of antidepressants from 1950s until today. *Current Pharmaceutical Design*, 15: 1563–86.

National Institute of Health. 2010. *Fact Sheet on the Human Genome Project*. Bethesda, Md: NIH.

Shorter, E. 1997. *A History of Psychiatry: From the Era of the Asylum to the Age of Prozac*. New York: John Wiley & Sons.

Teasdale, J., Williams, J., and Segal, Z. 2014. *The Mindful Way Workbook: An 8-Week Program to Free Yourself from Depression and Emotional Distress*. London: Guilford Press.

Chapter 6: Current controversies, future directions

Astin, J. 1998. Why patients use alternative medicine. *Journal of the American Medical Association*, 279: 1548–53.

Caron, M., and Gether, U. 2016. Structural biology: antidepressants at work. *Nature*, 532/7599: 320–1.

Goldacre, B. 2007. A kind of magic? *The Guardian*, 16 November 2007.

Jabr, F. 2011. Cache cab: taxi drivers' brains grow to navigate London's streets. *Scientific American*, 8 November.

Schatz, C. J. 1992. The developing brain. *Scientific American*, 267: 60–7.

Chapter 7: Depression in modern society

Foresight Group. 2008. *Mental Capital & Well-Being: Making the Most of Ourselves in the 21st Century*. London: Government Office for Science.

Gore, F., Bloem, P., Patton, G., Ferguson, J., Joseph, V., Coffey, C., Sawyer, S., and Mathers, C. 2011. Global burden of disease in young people aged 10–24 years: a systematic analysis. *Lancet*, 377/9783: 2093–102.

Jamison, K. 1993. *Touched with Fire*. New York: Free Press Paperbacks.

Layard, R. 2005. *The Depression Report: A New Deal for Depression and Anxiety Disorders*. London: London School of Economics & Political Science.

Murray, C., and Lopez, A. 1996. *The Global Burden of Disease: A Comprehensive Assessment of Mortality and Disability from Diseases, Injuries, and Risk Factors in 1990 and Projected to 2020*. Cambridge, Mass.: Harvard University Press on behalf of the World Health Organization.

Index

imaging 103
injuries 73
nervous system 48–51, 61
plasticity 99–104
surgery 73–5
transcranial magnetic stimulation (TMS) 73
brain-derived growth neurotrophic factor (BDNF) 102
bromide 70–1
Brown, George and Tyrell Harris 59–61
burden of disease 105–8
Burton, Robert 9–10

C

Cade, John 77–8
campaigns for awareness 115–16
Canon of Medicine (Avicenna) 4
Caspi 64–5
CBT *see* Cognitive Behaviour Therapy
Cerletti, Ugo 72
Charcot, Jean-Martin 18
chemical theories
of depression 47–8
of melancholia 10
childhood depression 32–4
Chinese medicine, traditional 8
chlorpromazine 76
Christianity in the Middle Ages 5–6
chromosomes 64
chronic depression 24, 25
chronic disease management 84–5
chronobiology 97–8
circadian rhythms 96–8
classification systems for mental disorders 24–6
clock genes 97
cognitive analytic therapy (CAT) 82
Cognitive Behaviour Therapy (CBT) 54, 81–2, 103

cognitive model (Beck) 54–8
complementary therapies 93–5
copycat suicides 44–5
corticotrophin releasing factor (CRF) 53
cortisol 53, 67, 95 *see also* stress hormones
counselling 45–6, 81, 92
creativity 116–21
Creativity's Melancholy Canvas (Schildkraut) 117
cultural variation 29
cyber-bullying 45

D

Dementia Praecox *see* schizophrenia
Deniker, Pierre and Jean Delay 76
diagnosing depression 21–6
criteria 26
under- and over-diagnoses 88–9
Diagnostic and Statistical Manual of Mental Disorders (DSM) 22–3, 24–5
Disability Adjusted Life Year (DALY) 106–8
divorce 32
dopamine 49
doshas 8 *see also* humours
drugs *see* medication
Durkheim, Émile 43–4
dysfunctional beliefs 56–8
dysthymia 24, 25

E

economic costs of depression 105–11, 113–14
education 35
ego (id, ego, and superego) 19
Einheitspsychose 12

Y